ROUTLEDGE LIBRARY EDITIONS:
AGRIBUSINESS AND LAND USE

I0121767

Volume 6

PRODUCERS AND CONSUMERS

PRODUCERS AND CONSUMERS

A Study in Co-Operative Relations

MARGARET DIGBY

Edited by
THE HORACE PLUNKETT FOUNDATION

Routledge
Taylor & Francis Group

LONDON AND NEW YORK

First published in 1928 by George Routledge & Sons Ltd

This edition first published in 2024
by Routledge
4 Park Square, Milton Park, Abingdon, Oxon OX14 4RN

and by Routledge
605 Third Avenue, New York, NY 10158

Routledge is an imprint of the Taylor & Francis Group, an informa business

© 1928 Margaret Digby

British Library Cataloguing in Publication Data
A catalogue record for this book is available from the British Library

ISBN: 978-1-032-48321-4 (Set)
ISBN: 978-1-032-48535-5 (Volume 6) (hbk)
ISBN: 978-1-032-48538-6 (Volume 6) (pbk)
ISBN: 978-1-003-38953-8 (Volume 6) (ebk)

DOI: 10.4324/9781003389538

Publisher's Note
The publisher has gone to great lengths to ensure the quality of this reprint but points out that some imperfections in the original copies may be apparent.

Disclaimer
The publisher has made every effort to trace copyright holders and would welcome correspondence from those they have been unable to trace.

PRODUCERS AND CONSUMERS

A STUDY IN CO-OPERATIVE RELATIONS

BY

MARGARET DIGBY

EDITED BY

THE HORACE PLUNKETT FOUNDATION

LONDON

GEORGE ROUTLEDGE & SONS, LTD.

BROADWAY HOUSE : 68–78 CARTER LANE, E.C.

1928

First Edition, October, 1928

PRINTED IN GREAT BRITAIN BY
BILLING AND SONS LTD., GUILDFORD AND ESHER

EDITORIAL NOTE

Two motives prompted the Horace Plunkett Foundation to initiate this study of co-operative relations between organised producers and consumers. One was to meet a growing demand for objective and comprehensive information on a subject which, in spite of the rising flood of co-operative literature, had not been dealt with in this manner, although the subject itself, as will be seen in the chapter on Policy, is by no means a new one. So untrodden was the road of original research, so variable and conflicting the few details to be obtained at second hand, that the author, to whom is due the entire credit for the clarity and conciseness of their presentation, spent the best part of a year in this young and virgin but already dense and darkling forest of co-operative business facts, collecting and collating her specimens. And as specimens only must be taken those instances of inter-trading which are specifically described; the network of non-profit-making organisation for the conveyance of food from field and orchard to the kitchen, though yet a light one, is already far too widely flung even in England to be displayed complete in a single volume.

The other motive was a desire to make a substantial contribution to the development of that economic theory which is ever at the back of the mind of the convinced co-operator. Again, referring to the chapter on Policy, the reader will be able to discern some of the changes which theory has undergone.   To those who hold, with the Members and Associates of the Foundation, that co-operative organisation of the producers of food is a necessary economic stage toward a better rural life, the significance of this contribution will be self-evident. Early theory did not foresee the economic urge which is pushing the agricultural producer to organise in his own social as well as economic interest. Progress has revealed a conflict unsuspected by the pioneer; any theory of the future will have to accept and resolve this material dualism of the movement.   Miss Digby has, in her concluding chapter, given some hints regarding a possible tendency in view of the facts presented; but the contribution is intentionally one of material rather than reflection.

On behalf of the Foundation it is desired to thank the members of public institutions who have helped in the compilation of this work, and members of co-operative organisations, whose assistance in many cases involved a laborious analysis of business records quite unnecessary (though sometimes, no doubt, illuminating) to their own office purposes.

K. WALTER,
Secretary.

CONTENTS

PRODUCERS AND CONSUMERS

INTRODUCTION

THE traditional methods of producing agricultural commodities, especially food, and distributing them to the consumer are in many ways wasteful and uneconomic, and do not give the best service either to producer or consumer. These methods have not been consciously thought out; they have developed spontaneously under the influence of variable economic, historical, and geographical circumstances, their immediate object being the profit of every individual concerned. Any economic structure extending over the gap between production and consumption is bound to be, architecturally speaking, a system of thrust and counter-thrust; but in the traditional relation between producer and consumer thrust and counter-thrust not only vary in strength from day to day, but bear no fixed relation to one another, so that the whole fabric is in perpetual disequilibrium. In its extremer forms occurs what is known as speculation. The instability is augmented by the anxiety of each person concerned to secure, irrespective of his fellows, his own profit and survival in the event of a crash.

The resultant evils are well known. The producer receives a return for his services which is inadequate to his standard of life, or even inadequate as an incentive to further sales or further production. Produce is destroyed, land is allowed to go out of cultivation. On the other hand, the consumer pays more than he can afford to do and yet maintain his standard of life, or he curtails consumption and goods are left upon the market. Both these processes, it is true, tend to right themselves in time, but they do so at the cost of much intermediate waste and loss. Even the middleman's position is precarious, though it may still be profitable.

Consumption is a single act. Production is a composite act, extending in time and involving a great variety of processes. In one sense, all those engaged in transport, warehousing, selling, are producers. There is, however, an actual tendency for distribution to disassociate itself from production and consumption, and to take up an intermediate position antagonistic to both. This is the position of the middleman. It is a key position, and one that he is suspected of abusing. At least he has turned the straight fight between producer and consumer into a three-cornered contest, and in the process obscured its issues and complicated its problems. Moreover, to both producers and consumers, his position is a No Man's Land which either may hope one day to occupy.

For many years attempts have been made to arrive at a more satisfactory system by the application of intelligent organisation to production and distribution for consumption, more especially by basing that organisation on the needs of communities rather than individuals. There are two main problems to be solved which stand in loose relation to one another. The first is the problem of economical handling, which is largely economy of labour, whether it be the labour of the ploughman or the grain broker, and to a certain extent the economy of capital. The second, perhaps the most important, and certainly the most difficult, is concerned with the old idea of the just price. It may be defined as the price which accords an equivalent standard of life to producer and consumer, but the application of that definition is one of great difficulty, and constitutes the ideal if not always the ostensible object of the movement to be described in this study.

This movement goes by the general name of co-operation, but it is in reality two movements which are concerned one with producers and the other with consumers, and are thus complementary rather than identical. In the middle of the nineteenth century, consumers in England and other European countries began to organise themselves into the familiar " Industrial Societies " which, under the management of the members, opened stores selling to members their daily necessaries, principally food. An attempt was made to achieve the just price by the abolition of profit, secured by distributing trading surplus to members in proportion to their purchases. In other words, members bought everything at cost price, while cost price itself was reduced by the society's bargaining power. This, obviously, is only a partial solution of the problem of the just price, as it takes no account of the producer. As the movement grew, the problem of economy of handling was also tackled with considerable success, through organisation on a large scale and through the elimination of wasteful competition. At the same time the movement pushed further into the debatable land of the middleman by organising a wholesale society to cater for the needs of the retail societies, and even went beyond it and became itself a producer in various departments.

The producers, of whom the most important were agricultural producers, were not far behind in organisation. They formed self-governing societies with the object of facilitating production and making it less costly to the producer, thus at the outset tackling the problems of both economy and the just price. These societies fulfilled various functions. They purchased agricultural requisites for their members—really a form of consumption, but of consumption for the purposes of production—they obtained credit and arranged insurance. Later they took a step more directly analogous to the activities of the consumers' societies, and organised the marketing of their members' produce. They, too, pushed into the middleman's territory with wholesale agencies and marts, and even planted retail stores beyond the consumers' frontier. Important as was their contribution to the determination of the just price, it was still partial, for it took no account of the consumer.

Producers' co-operation is to a very large extent a rural, and consumers' co-operation an urban, movement. This is especially the case in British countries. There is nothing in the character of the movement which makes this inevitable, though there are contributory causes which make it probable. In any case, it is a fact to be reckoned with.

Co-operation is a new element in economic life of an importance which it is difficult to exaggerate. In considering it, it is necessary to bear one or two points in mind. Firstly, great as the movement is, it has by no means yet supplanted private trade. The consumers of Great Britain who are members of a co-operative society and buy their food at its stores are between one-third and one-half of the population. As much as 80 per cent. of some of the exports of Denmark, New Zealand, and Ireland are the produce of farmers' co-operative societies. In many countries the proportion is less, but still considerable. It exists alongside and mingled with the older economic system, but it is increasing more rapidly than business conducted on any other principle. Secondly, though it has gone far to solving many major problems, it has created several minor ones of some perplexity. The great problems of economy and the just price cannot themselves be described as solved, but facts seem to show that they are at least on the way to a very interesting solution.

The two movements have started from opposite ends of the same economic process; they have shown themselves capable of controlling its ultimate phases, and have encroached successfully on the functions of the middleman. They are coming more and more to confront one another directly, to be conscious of one another's existence and of the element of conflict that is latent in their activities— the obvious but superficial conflict between the man who has something to sell and the man who wants to buy it. At the same time, both sides are beginning to be aware that, if there is a conflict, there is also an economic tie strong enough to constitute a community of interest, and that in any case a solution by conflict would be ruinous to both parties. This is prompting them to organise their mutual relations as they have organised their internal economy. In the following study an attempt is made to describe and discuss this latest development of co-operation.

CO-OPERATIVE POLICY

BESIDES being a subject of concrete developments in trading and organisation, agricultural co-operation has been, at least for the last sixty years, a matter of policy for various co-operative and certain other non-co-operative bodies. As the present and future relations of co-operative producers and consumers are largely affected by the past policy of the co-operative movement as a whole, it is worth outlining this policy as it has developed, in some cases touching on the formulation of outside opinion.

BRITISH POLICY

From its formation in 1869 onwards, the Congresses of the Co-operative Union (the educational and propagandist centre of the industrial movement) have been in the habit of discussing such subjects as land nationalisation, small-holdings, and co-operative farming, which, in early days, usually meant some scheme for owning and tilling land by co-operative colonies. At the Congress of 1882, a Canadian farmer co-operator was present who described the butter and cheese marketing organisations of his own country. In 1890 Sir Horace Plunkett spoke on agricultural co-operation in Ireland. During these years a thin trail of information runs through the Union's reports regarding industrial societies' agricultural undertakings, colony farms, and latterly, agricultural co-operative societies. The in-

6

dustrial societies' farms are rarely profitable, the colonies disappear altogether, but the agricultural co-operative societies increase slowly but steadily in number and importance.

In 1895 Mr. McInnes of the Lincoln Industrial Society read a paper on Co-operation and Agriculture, in which he described the success of his own society in penetrating into rural areas, organising agriculturists as consumers, and purchasing their produce. On the whole, he appeared opposed to the owning of farms by industrial societies; but he encouraged them to spread their influence into the country and to organise smallholders and producers generally both for marketing and for the purchase of seeds and other requirements. A resolution was passed requesting the United Board to formulate an agricultural co-operative program on the following points: (1) ownership of land by co-operative bodies, (2) the conditions of labour on the land, (3) the desirability of co-operative agriculture being carried out either by bodies of workers, special societies, or the existing distributive societies. A sub-committee was appointed to go into these matters and report to the next Congress (1896). They did so, recommending (1) that the Co-operative Union should encourage societies of smallholders and allotment-holders both for the purchase of requirements and the sale of their produce, (2) that distributive co-operative societies should not farm themselves unless they could absorb the produce of their own farms (this was probably a caution against " colony farm " projects), and (3) that the distributive societies should establish joint buying agencies for the purchase of agricultural produce from the source. This policy was approved by the Congress, and remitted to the sections and districts for discussion.

In 1898 the subject came up again. It was discussed by the Productive Committee of the Union, who brought forward a plan for the purchase of land by co-operative distributive societies, who would then lease it to co-operative societies of smallholders. Model rules were drafted. The proposal was approved by Congress held that year at Peterborough, and once more submitted to the societies for discussion. It does not seem to have awakened much interest or received much support either from them or from the Wholesales, to whom it was also submitted. A re-affirming resolution was passed in 1900. In the same year, the English Agricultural Organisation Society was formed, and began its work in close touch with the Co-operative Union, two representatives of the Union being members of its Board. A resolution in support of it was passed by Congress in 1903, endorsed in the following terms by the Congress of 1904: " Noting with satisfaction the growth of co-operation among agriculturists . . . and believing it desirable that a closer connection should exist . . . (the Congress) pledges itself to support the A.O.S. . . . and to use its influence to encourage trading between the C.W.S. and the farmers' societies." It further approved the Peterborough policy of co-operative land owning and sub-letting to smallholders. A detailed scheme for carrying out this last suggestion was circulated amongst the societies who, perhaps wisely, failed to respond. The same Congress had before it a report of the comparative failure of farming by distributive societies.

In 1906 a Joint Committee with the A.O.S. was appointed,

which concerned itself largely with problems of over-lapping. It reported to the Congress of 1907, which also passed a resolution welcoming the Small Holdings Act, and hoping that advantage might be taken of it to form co-operative societies. At the Congress of 1909, the Secretary of the A.O.S., Mr. Nugent Harris, read a paper on Agricultural Co-operation, and brought forward a scheme for inter-trading. A speaker from the C.W.S. followed, who proposed the formation of a C.W.S. Agricultural Department for the sale of seeds, feeding stuffs, etc. (a business already carried on to a limited extent), and the purchase of farm produce. He suggested the absorption of the existing Agricultural Federation in this body. He gave some account of C.W.S. buying methods, especially its sales of green fruit on commission for farmers. At this time the agricultural societies apparently sold more of certain types of produce than the C.W.S. could absorb. A resolution was passed affirming " that the time has come when the producer on the land should be brought closer to the consumer, and that therefore a concrete policy of co-operative distribution and supply in organised agriculture should be defined," and that a joint conference of the Union, C.W.S., and Joint Boards for Trade and Organisation should be called. This was done, and the Joint Conference in its turn adopted a resolution moved by a representative of the I.A.O.S. " That while it is desirable that the agricultural co-operative movement should be brought into closer business relations with the industrial co-operative movement, it is the opinion of the Conference that their relations should be so established as to develop the co-operative efficiency of agricultural societies, and encourage the spread of co-operation among agriculturists," and that for this purpose a sub-committee be appointed.

The sub-committee was formed, and eventually recommended as follows: (1) That every encouragement be given to farmers' organisations; (2) That such organisations should be federated, ultimately on a national scale, for trading purposes; (3) that all inter-co-operative trade should be through federations on both sides, " and such trade should be preferential and subject to a lower margin of profit " than external sales; (4) that competition between agricultural and industrial societies should be brought to an end; (5) that a meeting of C.W.S. buyers should be held to carry out these requirements. The last suggestion was put into practice immediately. The C.W.S. buyers met, and a discussion took place on butter, eggs, pigs, poultry, milk, corn, and cattle.

The Joint Conference was continued till November, 1913, when it was found that, while progress had been made in England and Wales, nothing had been done in Ireland, and definite hostility existed in Scotland. The Conference, therefore, decided virtually to suspend its activities while appointing a sub-committee for England and Wales formed of three representatives from the Farmers' Central Trading Board, three from the C.W.S., two from the Co-operative Union, and one from the A.O.S. This Committee reported to Congress of 1914, at which a paper on Inter-relations was also read by Mr. G. W. Russell. It contained the principal suggestion that the wholesale societies should make themselves as much suppliers for the agricultural as for the industrial movement.

The sub-committee for England and Wales continued to function through the years of the war. In 1915 a difficult situation was caused by the formation of the C.W.S. agricultural department, without consulting and in competition with, the existing Farmers' Central Trading Board. The latter body had been formed shortly before, after an effort to get the C.W.S. to form its own agricultural department, and had been performing many of the functions of an agricultural wholesale. The Farmers' Trading Board retaliated with a circular to farmers' societies cautioning them against recognising the C.W.S. agricultural department. The matter was discussed at several joint conferences; it was first proposed that the C.W.S. should trade through the Farmers' Trading Board, granting them preferential terms; the C.W.S. replied that they saw no necessity for the existence of the Farmers' Central Trading Board, and consequently could not see their way to grant them preferential terms. Discussion showed that some agricultural societies dealt with one body, some with the other. No method of accommodation was suggested; the alternatives before the Trading Board appeared to be absorption by the C.W.S. or complete and virtually hostile independence.

In 1916 the sub-committee only met once to discuss the policy of the C.W.S. in the purchase of milk and to urge that more business should be done with existing farmers' dairy societies. The attitude of the C.W.S. in requiring that all trade between farmers' societies and retail societies should pass through its own hands instead of going direct was also discussed. A request for further enlightenment on its plans was submitted to the C.W.S. The question of relations with the Farmers' Central Trading Board was not taken up again.   Later in the year the C.W.S. withdrew from the sub-committee.

By 1917 the sub-committee had ceased to function.   The subject of co-operation and agriculture came up once more at Congress, but under the pressure of war conditions the discussion took a different turn.   It was resolved, " That this Congress considers it advisable in the interests of the consumer that farming be undertaken by distributive societies, either individually or in federation, as a means of controlling prices and supplies of food-stuffs and raw materials."

In 1918 a plan was agreed upon between the Wholesales and a number of local societies, by which allotment-holders could bulk their orders through the local societies to the Wholesale Societies' agricultural departments.   At the same time, the widening breach between the Union and the A.O.S. was revealed in a resolution passed at Congress which stated that, " In view of the fact that the agriculturists are organising themselves and forming co-operative societies, and that such societies would cause overlapping and un-necessary officialism, this Congress calls upon the Co-opera-tive Union to take prompt action to bring about the utilisa-tion of the present machinery for dealing with their produce."

By 1919 the breach appeared complete.   The Farmers' Central Trading Board was transformed into the Agricultural Wholesale Society.   The A.O.S. removed the two repre-sentatives of the Union from its Board of Governors, and the Union withheld its subscription from the A.O.S.   In view of this situation an emergency resolution was passed at Congress instructing the Union "to consider the advisability of setting up a special agricultural committee for the purpose of organising co-operative societies for small farmers." At the same time a measure of success was reported in the schemes for organising and assisting smallholders.

As long ago as 1914, Congress had instructed the Union to carry out a complete survey of the movement. This was done, and sections of the survey appeared from year to year during the war. In 1920 a special Congress was called to consider the result. The Survey, in dealing with agriculture, sketched the past of the two movements and their growing hostility to one another. It made it clear that the Union had ceased to wish for collaboration with the A.O.S. and that it recommended the affiliation of small-holding societies to itself, the absorption of the A.W.S. in the agricultural department of the C.W.S., and the affiliation of farmers' societies to a special C.W.S. section. At the same time it advocated inter-trading and some form of joint machinery to discuss difficult questions, such as those of price. An agricultural section of the Union, with a subsection for allotment societies, was proposed for England, and joint councils for Ireland and Scotland. In districts where no farmers' society existed, retail societies were recommended to form departments for the sale of agricultural requirements. The Survey also considered at some length the subject of farming by the retail societies, and recommended the purchase of colonial estates by the C.W.S. It rather deprecated extensive agricultural operations by the C.W.S. in this country, and declared in favour of purchase from organised farmers, at the same time proposing a pooling of the purchases of raw materials by the C.W.S. and the the productive societies.   It also threw out a suggestion that the C.W.S. should lease land to working farmers in order that they should produce for the co-operative market.   .

By the end of 1919, however, relations with the A.O.S. had been resumed to the extent of a joint conference, at which problems of overlapping were discussed without any very definite results.   It was suggested, however, that the two movements might collaborate in getting the limit of co-operative shareholding raised to £500, in maintaining the rights of co-operative societies to tax-remission, and in withstanding the attacks of private traders.   At Congress a speaker urged the absorption of the A.O.S. and its member societies by the Co-operative Union.

During the two following years no further developments took place.   In 1923 the Linlithgow Committee on the price of agricultural produce began its sittings.   The Co-operative Union failed to secure representation, but it gave evidence before the Committee.   In the following year, the Committee issued its report, which contained the following passages:

" A number of societies send their milling wheat direct to the mills.   This method of trading is stated to be actively developing, and inasmuch as the sole parties concerned are producers on the one hand and consumers on the other, it represents the complete integration of the marketing and distributive processes."

" The establishment of trading relations between the industrial co-operative movement and producers co-operative organisations is a development that should be continuously explored."

Some of the recommendations of the Report, including the sections bearing on co-operation, were adopted by the Ministry of Agriculture and Fisheries. The Co-operative Movement was granted representation on the Milk Advisory Committees which were set up in England and Scotland. In the same year an Agricultural Credits Act was passed, which, however, failed to encourage the formation of co-operative credit societies. At Congress (1924) a resolution was passed which (1) endorsed the Linlithgow recommendation on inter-trading, (2) welcomed the Agricultural Credits Act, (3) re-affirmed the 1919 Congress decision to establish an agricultural section of the Union, and instructed the Board to proceed with the matter.

A little later in the year the Conference on Agricultural Co-operation in the British Empire was held at Wembley, convened by the Horace Plunkett Foundation. One session was devoted to the discussion of the relations between co-operative producers and consumers. An address was given by Sir Thomas Allen, in which he sketched the relations of the C.W.S. with agriculture as they existed in 1924. In the discussion that followed, the work of the New Zealand Producers, Ltd., was described; other speakers from both sides of the movement stressed the separate functions of the two and the dangers, firstly, of commercial overlapping and, secondly, of political friction. A good deal of discussion centred on the particular point at which the product should leave the hands of the producer and pass to those of the consumer, as well as the even more difficult question of price-fixing. The possibility of the industrial movement financing agricultural co-operation was also mentioned. At the conclusion, the following resolution was passed:

1. That until some complete information on the cost of agricultural production is available, the prices of agricultural produce must continue to be fixed by a process of bargaining.

2. That the immediate task before co-operators is to enable bargaining to take place more and more directly between the organisations of co-operating producers and those of co-operating consumers, so as gradually to eliminate the control now exercised by the middleman.

3. That all federations of agricultural co-operative societies should endeavour to establish close inter-trading relations with the Consumers' Wholesale Society.

Throughout this and the following year the Co-operative Union devoted a good deal of attention to agricultural questions, their activities including the part taken by their representatives at the International Co-operative Congress at Ghent, which will be mentioned later. A sub-committee, in consultation with the Wholesales, was appointed to act along the lines indicated by the Linlithgow Report. At this time the Agricultural Wholesale Society went into liquidation, and the Agricultural Organisation Society ceased to exist, its functions being transferred to a committee of the National Farmers' Union. A joint conference was held by the National Farmers' Union and the Co-operative Union, but the discussion was principally confined to milk contracts. At the same time the Union felt the lack of a distinctive Agricultural Section, and with the concurrence of the Wholesales, decided to carry out the resolution passed at the preceding Congress. In March, 1925, the Union definitely constituted an Agricultural Department, with the following functions:

1. To organise and carry out propaganda and education of both farmers' and industrial co-operative societies, with a view to furthering the development of inter-trading relationships between the co-operative movement and agriculturists.

2. To collect agricultural statistics and information generally relating to their agricultural experiences from co-operative societies, and to be in a position to give advice to such societies engaged in farming.

For this purpose it was proposed to appoint a qualified man to the head of the department, with a staff under him. The Co-operative Union met representatives of the C.W.S., who approved the scheme and agreed to collaborate. The proposal was submitted to Congress in the same year. It was introduced by Mr. A. V. Alexander and supported by others, though discussion showed that not all societies were unreservedly in favour of the policy. The following resolution, however, was passed unanimously:

" This Congress welcomes the establishment of an Agricultural Department of the Co-operative Union, and instructs the Central Board and the Parliamentary Committee to do all in their power to develop the Department to the full, both for the help of societies with agricultural interests and to establish direct trading relationships with the agricultural industry. The Congress further expresses the hope that all societies in membership with it will co-operate to secure the success of these objects."

2

The Department as constituted was placed in charge of a joint committee of three representatives of the Co-operative Union, and three of the C.W.S. An organiser was appointed whose duties were to visit agricultural and industrial societies, promote good feeling and inter-trading, induce agricultural societies to become members of the Co-operative Union and the Wholesale, and advise industrial societies on the management of their farms. The Department also met the National Farmers' Union on several occasions, and sent a speaker to address a conference of agricultural co-operative societies convened by the N.F.U. on inter-trading. Some evidence of the progress of thought on these lines may be found in the N.F.U. interim Report on Marketing published in 1927.

"County branch executives should bear in mind the desirability of arranging conferences with distributive organisations to examine any special aspects of marketing organisation affecting the County Branch area or any particular locality within that area."

A special committee on co-operative farming was also appointed by the Union and sat during 1925-26. Its attention was mainly occupied by the technicalities of farming, but its report alludes sympathetically to agricultural co-operation, and the following points are included in its recommendations:

"That the Agricultural Department Committee be requested to consider the devising of suitable machinery for linking together organised producers and organised consumers.

"That the attention of the Agricultural Department Committee be called to the desirability of securing the establishment of joint councils representing farmers' societies and consumers' societies, to consider the standardisation of produce, the cultivation of good relationships, and of trade between the two types of organisation and the determination of a price basis for transferred produce."

The work of the Department was continued through 1926-7. There was no great development in joint work with the N.F.U., and some of the industrial societies showed hostility to the admission of agricultural societies to the Union. At the same time the organiser attended shows, prepared a pamphlet on *British Co-operation and British Agriculture*, and addressed a number of conferences of agricultural societies on inter-relations and inter-trading.

In 1927 the organiser resigned in order to take up another position in the movement and, soon after, the work of the Department received a more serious check through the withdrawal of the C.W.S. from the joint committee. A special sub-committee considered the position and recommended that a committee consisting of Union representatives only should be appointed to carry on the work already planned out, that a new organiser should be appointed, " that a separate Agricultural Department of the Union should be established to which agricultural societies should be admitted," and that the C.W.S. should be invited to reconsider its withdrawal. The C.W.S., however, merely confirmed its decision, and in November, 1927, the United Board of the Union recommended the abolition of the Agricultural Department. Vigorous protests were, however, immediately raised by some of the Sectional Boards, and by many others in the movement. Finally, early in 1928, it was decided to keep the Department in being, and to adopt the scheme of work outlined above, with the exception of the clauses relating to the C.W.S.; a fresh organiser was very shortly appointed. This decision was confirmed at the Co-operative Congress of 1928. The agricultural programme of the Co-operative Party, which included a paragraph on the encouragement of inter-trading, was also adopted, as was the detailed resolution on agricultural co-operation contained in the report of the International Co-operative Alliance.

This is the position as it stands in England to-day. It may be well to state briefly the progress of opinion on the same subject in the international sphere.

INTERNATIONAL POLICY

The International Co-operative Alliance, a body consisting principally of national consumers' societies, but also including a number of agricultural organisations, held its first Congress in London in 1895. This Congress, " recognising the gravity of the agricultural crisis throughout Europe," recommended the adoption of co-operative methods of agriculture and the establishment of associations " for agricultural supply and sale of farm produce, agricultural banks, profit-sharing farms, etc."

In the following year the International Congress reaffirmed this recommendation, adding that, " with a view to stimulating industrial and agricultural co-operation . . . it (was) desirable to establish in all countries committees for the organisation . . . of international commercial relations between co-operative societies . . . Co-operative distributive societies . . . should give preference in the furnishing of their goods at equal prices and quality to industrial and agricultural co-operative societies . . . and productive co-operative societies should accord best prices to distributive societies."

Soon after, a proposal was put forward in France for a national co-operative productive exchange. The International Congress of 1897 noted this development with approval, and hoped that the idea might be extended internationally. At the same time the Congress laid down its own policy in still greater detail, declaring: " That . . . the interests of the agricultural population demand the organisation of co-operative societies in which all branches of the movement should be centralised with the exception of credit . . . that the services of general interest ought to include the collective purchase of raw material, seeds, manure . . . also the joint purchase of machinery . . . also all articles necessary to the material needs of the population. . . that the collective sale of agricultural produce be undertaken as far as possible by centralising products for sale *en bloc* at large markets or by auction."

The Congress did not meet again till 1900, when it recommended the appointment of an international commission of producers' and consumers' agricultural and industrial co-operative organisations to promote inter-relations. It further recommended the formation of a similar commission in each country.

In 1902 the Congress contented itself with passing a resolution recommending the employment of co-operative funds for settling small cultivators on the land. In 1904 an unfortunate quarrel arose between the industria and agricultural organisations within the Alliance on the question of state aid. The consumers' organisations clung to their traditional objection to all forms of state aid to the movement, and the agricultural organisations, who took the opposite view, thereupon seceded from the Alliance. They formed an International of their own which, however, came to an end in the War. The resolution of the 1904 Congress seems to reflect the new attitude to agricultural co-operation of a Congress of industrial co-operators alone. It was resolved: " That this Congress, being of opinion that distributive co-operation . . . is as urgently needed in rural districts . . . as it is in towns . . . calls upon co-operators in all countries to contribute to . . . its establishment and extension."

The next two Congresses did little more than give agricultural co-operation a perfunctory place in the scheme of things, and throw out a vague suggestion that there should be one C.W.S. in each country for both agricultural and industrial co-operative societies.

At the Congress of 1913, however, a representative of the German Co-operative Union read a paper on " The Direct Exchange of Goods between Consumers', Agricultural and other Productive Societies," and submitted a scheme for the sale of agricultural produce by producers to consumers and the sale of agricultural requirements by consumers to producers on a local, national, and international scale. The war caused a long break in international co-operative relations, but when the next Congress was held in 1921, the Congress expressed itself as follows: " That commercial relations between the co-operative organisations of various countries will not only serve the general good by eliminating middlemen's profits, but will also lay a strong foundation for a world economic system in which the spirit of strife and competition will have no place. For this purpose it recommends the establishment of direct relations as between country and country and within each country, between organised consumers and agricultural producers' organisations, and it counts on the central authorities of the International Co-operative Alliance to unite all the co-operative organisations of the whole world."

In 1924 another attempt was made to define and elaborate co-operative policy. The tendency of the resolution is to describe co-operation in its widest terms, to unify its various manifestations, and to find a place for all aspirations and activities connected with it. The passage relating to agriculture runs as follows: " It is desirable that organic relations should be established between distributive and agricultural co-operative organisations, with a view to the local and national consolidation of the interests of industrial and agricultural countries, on the basis of mutual respect for each other's conditions of life and work."

At this Congress Sir Thomas Allen also made a declaration of some importance when he said: " I do not hold that it is the primary task of the consumers' movement either as a wholesale organisation or a retail institution to undertake in any extensive degree agricultural production. I believe that is best left to agricultural societies. But what I do feel is that the agricultural productive co-operative societies should arrange the closest relationship with organised distribution for the marketing of products."

In 1924 the International Co-operative Wholesale Society,

Ltd., was formed by the union of existing national Whole-sales. It has continued in existence ever since, though it has not engaged in actual trading, and its services have been principally of an advisory and statistical nature. Its members, except for the U.S.S.R., have very slight agri-cultural interests. Co-operative Banking and Insurance Committees set up by the International Co-operative Alliance are also in existence and, though the agricultural movement has not at present seen its way to be represented on them, they indicate lines along which inter-relations may at some time be developed.

At the International Congress of 1927, " Relations between Agricultural and Consumers' Co-operative Societies " was once more treated as a separate subject. A programme of development was adopted, of which the following are the principal points:

1. Inter-trading between producers' and consumers' organisations shall be further developed.

2. Both consumers' and agricultural societies shall so arrange their administration that the products which they offer shall bear a minimum charge for expenses.

3. Mixed committees or undertakings jointly administered shall be appointed.

4. Co-operative saving shall be revived and co-operative banks established, so that consumers' and agricultural societies can render themselves independent of private capitalist banks.

5. Joint educational institutions shall be recommended.

6. The two forms of association shall jointly defend the cause of the societies in matters of legislation, administration, and justice.

One of the points raised in discussion was the desirability of the return of the agricultural organisations to membership of the Alliance.

Other international bodies have been interested in the same question. In 1926 the International Institute of Agriculture at Rome issued a " Preliminary Report on the sale of Agricultural Produce by Producers' Co-operative Societies to Consumers' Co-operative Societies," which contained useful information but has not yet been followed up by any more comprehensive survey.

Finally, the question came up before the League of Nations and the International Labour Office. The International Economic Conference held in May, 1927, as well as the Preparatory Committee that preceded it, included amongst its members several co-operators appointed as experts. The International Labour Office also prepared valuable documentation, especially on the co-operative handling of wheat and dairy produce. The business before the Conference was divided into three headings—Commerce, Industry and Agriculture; under the latter appeared the subsidiary heading, "Development of international collaboration between producers' and consumers' organisations, including the different systems of co-operative organisation." The Conference summed up the result of its deliberations in a series of general and special resolutions. The general resolution on agriculture contained the following passage:

" That . . . the organisation of agriculturists should be continued along the lines of association and combination; it may with advantage be supplemented by agreements between agricultural and consumers' co-operative societies."

This was followed by a special resolution cordially approving agricultural co-operation as a system, and making the following specific suggestions:

" (ii.) Agricultural Co-operative societies will contribute to a still greater rationalisation of economic life in proportion as they develop their relations with the consumers' co-operative societies. Direct commercial relations between producers and consumers, and between associations of producers and consumers, eliminate superfluous intermediaries, and, when they are sufficiently widespread result in the establishment of prices which are advantageous to both parties. In addition to material profit, there is a moral advantage; by direct commercial relations producers and consumers learn to know each other, and to take account of the special requirements and characteristics of the other party. The producers' and consumers' co-operative societies learn to appreciate the value of direct relations in accordance with their common principles. The clear realisation of the possibility of mutual collaboration and mutual confidence in business transactions are essential to a practical solution of the question of direct commercial relations between producers' agricultural co-operative societies and consumers' co-operative societies—a question which has for a long time been settled in theory.

" The effort to achieve practical results should be furthered on the part of agriculture by production of articles of specific quality and uniform type; on the part of the consumers' co-operative societies by the determination to buy agricultural produce as far as possible from the agricultural producers' co-operative societies. . . .

" Effective collaboration, if need be in the form of common undertakings, will be the easier of realisation if the producers' and consumers' co-operative societies of the different countries are already nationally organised in common economic committees. . . .

" (iii.) International agreements between co-operative agricultural organisations with regard to a number of products might be of value in placing markets on a sound basis, in regularising production, and in stabilising prices at levels satisfactory from the point of view of the balance between production and consumption. Such international agreements, to attain their aims, require loyal collaboration with the national and international co-operative consumers' organisations by the establishment of regular business channels and long-term contracts.

" (iv.) These efforts of agricultural and consumers' co-operative organisations should be encouraged and furthered by the creation of a committee representing national and international co-operative organisations of agriculturists and of consumers—a committee which should be entrusted with the establishment of a programme of research and documentation, as well as with the task of elucidating the lessons taught by past experience, with a view to bringing about new achievements."

Among its general recommendations the Conference suggested the perpetuation of a committee under the auspices of the League of Nations to deal especially with economic questions. The suggestion was adopted, and the Consultative Economic Committee, on which the co-operative movement was represented, held its first meeting in the spring of 1928. Dr. Hermes, the principal representative of Germany, put forward two subjects for early consideration by the Committee:

1. Organisation of markets with a view to their being placed on a sound basis, and with a view to the distribution

and marketing of agricultural produce and the stabilisation of prices.

2. Rôle of agricultural co-operation—production and consumption—in this organisation.

It was further pointed out that " the examination of the highly important problem of the direct relations between producers' co-operative societies and consumers' societies should, no doubt, be dealt with here. . . . We think that this difficult problem should be examined from the practical point of view, and that an attempt should be made to ascertain how in particular direct agreements between producers' and consumers' co-operative societies may be promoted under an economic system in which prices are fixed, independently of these societies, by free competition and the operation of the law of supply and demand."

It may be mentioned that the International Economic Conference had already had a sequel of some national interest in a series of meetings held in London by the League of Nations Union, at which the work of the International Conference was reviewed. A session was devoted to the agricultural recommendations of the conference, and the case for inter-trading between agricultural and consumers' organisations was discussed.

It may be observed from the foregoing narrative, that the idea of agricultural co-operation and its relation to the consumers' movement has been presented to the minds of co-operators for many years, that with the passage of time it has changed, developed, and crystallised, and that with the growth of an actual agricultural co-operative movement and existing inter-relations, it has descended from the realms of theory and been increasingly moulded by facts. In recent years it has come to occupy the attention not merely of co-operators, but also of politicians and economists, and to be considered as an international rather than a national question. It is the purpose of this study to review the facts of the situation as it exists to-day. In the last chapter an attempt will be made to sum up the whole position, and to indicate the conclusions which experience as well as theory suggest.

CO-OPERATIVE PRODUCTION IN THE BRITISH EMPIRE

IN many countries the development of co-operative production or co-operative consumption has far out-distanced its complementary movement. In many, especially in Europe, they are of nearly equal strength, and their mutual relations are frequently worth study. But as a subject for a survey of this kind the British Empire is unapproached in interest, except, possibly, by the Soviet Union. Within it both movements have developed to a high degree of completeness in most varied conditions; they are evolving very important inter-relations which are all the more interesting because they bear in many instances the character of international trade. It is also, in many respects, a self-contained area.

It is a commonplace of the economy of the British Empire that, as concerns agricultural commodities, Great Britain is the centre of consumption and the Overseas Dominions of production. It is not entirely true of agricultural commodities as a whole, for British farming is still an important source of supplies, but it is true with less qualification of commodities co-operatively handled. This is not to say that there is no agricultural co-operation in Great Britain. There s much, and it is increasing, but on the whole it is organised for farmers' supply rather than for marketing, and the volume of goods which passes through its hands to the consumer is still small. On the other hand, consumers' co-operation in the Overseas Dominions is even less considerable. In Australia, Canada, New Zealand, South Africa, and the Irish Free State, the movements are all too small to have any serious effect on the market at present, whatever their development may be in the future. There is also a limited amount of distribution by co-operative producers direct to unorganised consumers. In Northern Ireland a flourishing consumers' movement exists, but as this is almost confined to the small industrial area of Belfast, the position resembles that in Great Britain.

It is useful to take the Dominions one by one, and consider how they stand as co-operative producers and exporters.

CANADA

GRAIN.—The most important co-operative export of Canada is wheat. A large proportion of the wheat of the three prairie provinces is controlled by three provincial Wheat Pools, of which the Alberta Pool was started in 1923, and the Saskatchewan and Manitoba Pools in 1924. In 1924 a joint selling agency was formed, " The Canadian Wheat Producers, Ltd.," generally known as the Canadian Wheat Pool. The Pool has export offices in Calgary, Vancouver, Toronto, New York, Paris, and London, as well as thirty-six other foreign agencies. The following figures will indicate the growth of the Pool and the extent of its operations.

Acreage under Wheat sending to Pool.

1925   ..   ..   14,300,000, or 67 per cent. of total.
1927   ..   ..   15,500,000.

Membership of Pool.

1925 .. 127,200.
1927 .. 140,000, or nearly 60 per cent. of wheat growers.

	Total Canadian Wheat Crop (Bushels).	Crop handled by Pool (Bushels).	Percentage.	Value $.
1923–4	474,199,000	34,218,980	7 per cent.	33,000,000
1924–5	262,097,000	81,670,305	31 per cent.	129,000,000
1925–6	411,375,700	187,361,240	45 per cent.	251,000,000
1926–7	—	179,785,739	—	231,000,000
1927–8[1]	—	198,204,374	—	—

1926-7	Wheat handled by Pool	179,785,739
	Home sales	55,650,431
	Export to twenty-four countries, 28 per cent. to Great Britain	124,135,308

This may be compared with the total wheat export for Canada for the two previous years:

1925 .. .. 142,975,859 bushels.
1926 .. .. 186,287,041 ,,

In 1925 the wheat handled by the Pool was equal to two-thirds of the total export, and a quarter of the world's wheat trade. In 1927 the Pool controlled over 67 per cent. of the Canadian export surplus. In 1926 it handled 80 per cent. of all the Canadian wheat sold in France. In the same year it was stated " that 65 per cent. of wheat marketing by the Central selling agency was handled entirely apart from the grain exchanges." The largest purchasers after Great Britain are Italy, Holland, Germany, Belgium, France and Japan.

The Pool also handled coarse grains to the following amounts in 1926-27:

[1] As at May 15, 1928.

				Bushels.
Oats	..	..	..	6,466,317
Barley	..	..	..	12,338,261
Flax	..	..	..	1,418,274
Rye	..	..	..	2,559,126
				22,781,978

FRUIT AND VEGETABLES.—The marketing of fruit and vegetables is organised to a very considerable extent. The principal centres of co-operative activity are: Nova Scotia (mainly fruit—in 1925, 40 per cent. of the apples were co-operatively marketed); Ontario (fruit, but also potatoes and turnips); New Brunswick (apples); Alberta (potatoes); British Columbia (fruit and a proportion of vegetables). In 1924 about 80 per cent. of the fruit crop in British Columbia was in the hands of co-operative organisations. The brokerage business was controlled by the growers, who had agencies in Great Britain and the United States. The Associated Fruit Growers of British Columbia sell annually goods worth on an average $3,000,000, of which $500,000 worth are vegetables. Measured in bulk this is equivalent to 4,000 car-loads, of which 800 are of vegetables and 3,200 of fruit. Of fruit alone 750 car-loads are exported, 500 to Great Britain.

The total export of Canadian fruit in 1927-28 was 950,000 barrels, of which 305,000, or 32 per cent., were co-operatively handled. Of these 275,000 went to Great Britain.

BUTTER AND CHEESE.—The total production and export of Canadian Creamery butter and factory cheese in 1925 was as follows:

	Produced.	Exported.
Butter ..	.. 169,494,967 lbs.	26,971,840 lbs.
Cheese ..	.. 177,139,113 ,,	142,721,600 ,,

3

It is not easy to give the co-operative percentage of these sales, but the following figures are of some interest. Co-operative butter and cheese factories are distributed through the provinces in the following proportions: Quebec, 223; Ontario, 189; Prince Edward Island, 23; Saskatchewan, 22; Alberta, 13; British Columbia, 12; New Brunswick, 11; Manitoba, 9; Nova Scotia, 7. The Saskatchewan Co-operative Creameries produced 4,850,000 lbs. of butter in 1923, and the Manitoba Co-operative Dairies 1,637,000 lbs. in 1927. Cheese-making is confined to Ontario and Quebec. The Quebec Federated Co-operative has a cheese and butter department which in 1923 handled 138,420 boxes of butter (about 7,750,000 lbs.) and 206,741 boxes of cheese. The United Dairymen's Co-operative, Ontario, markets about 17,000,000 lbs. annually, as well as about 2,500,000 lbs. of butter (figures for 1925). In 1927 this Association marketed cheese to the value of $2,000,600 ; about 90 per cent. of this was exported to Great Britain, 5 per cent. to the U.S.A., and the remainder sold locally.

WOOL.—The estimated wool clip of Canada in 1924 was 15,511,719 lbs. The Canadian Co-operative Wool Growers handled 2,506,326 lbs., or 16 per cent. Of this 655,500 lbs. was from Ontario and 68,000 lbs. from Alberta. In addition, the Quebec Federated Co-operative sold 18,600 lbs. of wool. In the following year the Co-operative Societies sold about 25 per cent. of the total Canadian clip, two-thirds was exported to the U.S.A., and a certain proportion also to Great Britain. Some of the wool is made up into textiles and returned to the members of the Association. The sales of the Canadian Co-operative Wool Growers for 1927 are as follows:

		Lbs.
Alberta		1,492,181
Manitoba and Saskatchewan ..		661,262
British Columbia		269,479
Ontario		651,989
Nova Scotia		61,175
Quebec		90,590
Prince Edward Island		29,986
New Brunswick		17,994
	Total ..	3,274,656
Carry over from 1926 ..	..	1,293,197
	Total ..	4,567,853

About 44 per cent. was exported to England, some of it for resale on the Continent. Sales in Canada itself amounted to 39 per cent., and the remainder was exported to the U.S.A. The exports in this year were, on the whole, unusually large.

HONEY.—In 1926, 85 per cent. of the total production of honey was co-operatively marketed and largely exported to Great Britain, Holland and Germany. Production is almost confined to Ontario and Quebec, and the largest organisation concerned is the Ontario Honey Producers. In 1927-28 this organisation sold 5,550,570 lbs. of honey, value $578,303. Of this 2,056,041 lbs., or 37 per cent., was exported. Only 495,534 lbs., or approximately a quarter of the exports, came to England.

EGGS.—In 1923 about 20 million eggs were handled co-operatively, but these do not form a large proportion of the total production. At the present moment the export of Canadian eggs of any kind to England is very slight.

LIVE STOCK.—Live stock in Canada is not handled co-operatively to any great extent. In the year 1923-24,

278,650 head of stock were marketed by co-operative
organisations in the three provinces of Alberta, Saskatchewan and Quebec, and in the following year the co-operative
associations of Ontario sold 6,212 car-loads of stock.

FEDERATION MARKETING.—Before going on to deal with
the other Dominions, mention should be made of the Overseas Farmers' Federation, Ltd., a co-operative marketing
organisation with its headquarters in London. This body
was formed in 1920 by the Australian Producers' Wholesale
Co-operative Federation, the Farmers' Co-operative Wholesale Federation of New Zealand, Ltd., and the Federated
Farmers' Co-operative Association of South Africa, Ltd.,
who are the sole shareholders. The company is engaged
in the marketing and distribution of produce, including
wheat, butter, cheese, eggs, honey, grain, dried fruits, maize,
meat and wool, in Great Britain and the Continent, and in
the combined purchasing of agricultural and domestic
requirements for export to the Dominions it represents.
The company does not trade but carries on its business on a
commission basis. In 1927 its business reached about
£14,250,000, of which the greater proportion represented
sales of Australian wheat. The company is also the London
agent of the Co-operative Insurance Company of Australia
and the Farmers' Co-operative Insurance Association of New
Zealand. It has no business relations with the co-operative
organisations of Canada, but it is in frequent consultation
with the Canadian associations, especially the Wheat Pools.
It has no connections outside the British Empire.

AUSTRALIA

The position in Australia differs from that of Canada in that the co-operative export of numerous commodities is concentrated in the hands of the Australian Producers' Wholesale Co-operative Federations, Ltd., which is itself one of the founders of the Overseas Farmers' Federations, Ltd. The position, however, is somewhat complicated, as a considerable proportion of the produce collected, and in the case of commodities like butter, manufactured by co-operative organisations, though exported by them, is sold through proprietary channels, while in a few cases the produce of private persons is exported under co-operative auspices. In 1927-28 the Australian Producers' Wholesale did a trade of £13,250,000; this sum does not, however, include all Australian co-operative produce passing to the European market through the hands of the Overseas Farmers.

WHEAT.—As in Canada, wheat is the largest item of co-operative export. In 1925-26 the total Australian production was 114,504,392 bushels, value £35,723,949, of which 47 per cent. was exported, 19 per cent. to Great Britain.

The next year's crop was 160,852,369 bushels, handled by Co-operative Wheat Pools as follows:

	Bushels.	*Percentage of Total Crop.*
New South Wales	8,500,000	25
Victoria	11,721,504[1]	25
S. Australia	8,688,543	43
W. Australia	24,017,292[2]	80
Queensland	1,799,263[3]	100
Commonwealth	54,726,602	33

[1] Estimated—possibly less.

[2] Includes 12 per cent. sold co-operatively but not pooled. In all about 87 per cent. of Western Australian wheat exports were sold co-operatively. [3] Marketing Board Pool—no export.

DAIRY PRODUCE.—The production of Australian butter in the year 1925-26 was 273,313,685 lbs., of which 35 per cent. was exported, about 90 per cent. of the export being to Great Britain.[1] The production of cheese is much smaller, amounting in the same year to 28,799,320 lbs., of which 21 per cent. was exported. The exact production of eggs is less easy to determine, as they are usually grouped for statistical purposes with poultry; the export, however, is 18,380,928 eggs, which would not appear to be more than about 2 per cent. of the total production. The bulk of the dairy produce comes from New South Wales, Victoria, and Queensland. About 80 per cent. or more of these commodities is co-operatively produced, but not more than 30 per cent. is exported through the Overseas Farmers' Federations. The rest goes through private agencies. From the co-operative point of view butter takes the first place in order of importance, eggs second, and cheese third. A Dairy Produce Control Board is in existence, but it does not engage in actually marketing. Its functions are mainly advisory and supervisory; it arranges freights and insures cargoes.[2]

There are considerable Australian exports of condensed milk, but these do not appear to be co-operatively handled.

FRUIT.—Dried fruit is exported to the amount of 55,428,846 lbs., value £1,463,417. Most of the growers are

[1] Australian butter forms an important item in British butter imports, amounting to about 20 per cent. of the total, and ranking after Danish and New Zealand.

[2] Another form of concerted action in marketing is the Patterson scheme, by which a 1d. per pound is levied on all butter produced in order to furnish a bounty of 3d. per pound on butter exported.

organised co-operatively (the Dried Fruit Association includes 90 per cent. of the Australian Currant Growers), but only about 33 per cent. of exports pass through the hands of the Overseas Farmers' Federations. Canned fruit is also produced, but not sold, co-operatively, and there are considerable exports of fresh fruit by co-operatively organised growers, of which a large proportion is sold through the Overseas Farmers.

SUGAR.—The entire cane sugar crop of Queensland, valued in 1925-26 at £6,354,625, is handled by a co-operative marketing board and about 80 per cent. exported. In Queensland not only all the above-mentioned commodities, but also cotton, maize, arrowroot, pigs, canary seed, peanuts, and broom millet are dealt with by co-operative marketing boards, but with the exception of cotton, the value handled is not considerable, nor do sales to any appreciable extent take place through the Overseas Farmers' Federations.

MEAT AND WOOL.—These commodities, especially wool, are amongst the most important exports of Australia, but they are scarcely touched by co-operative organisations. The Overseas Farmers' Federations handles a small quantity of meat on behalf of Co-operative Associations. Wool is handled by eleven large brokers, one of whom conducts business on lines which are to a certain extent co-operative in character. Nearly all wool is sold by auction in Australia prior to export. A very small proportion is handled by the Overseas Farmers' Federations.

New Zealand

The co-operative position in New Zealand differs as regards exports from the position both in Canada and Australia. It is represented in the Overseas Farmers' Federations by the New Zealand Farmers' Co-operative Wholesale Federation, one of its founders, but this body, although a regular exporter of butter and cheese, controls a very small proportion of the co-operative output of these commodities, which are mainly handled by two other principal exporting organisations unconnected with the Overseas Farmers' Federations. On the other hand, the latter body also receives shipments of other co-operative produce of kinds not handled by the New Zealand Farmers' Federation.

Butter and Cheese.—The export of New Zealand butter in 1926 was valued at £8,695,188, and that of cheese at £5,939,359. In 1925 it was stated that 80 per cent. of production and 92 per cent. of export was co-operatively organised. In 1928, 500 out of the existing 518 butter factories (96 per cent.) were co-operative. A small export trade is carried on through the Farmers' Federation abovementioned, which consigns to the Overseas Farmers in London. The New Zealand Co-operative Dairy Company which in 1925 controlled 32 per cent. of production, probably now, as member of a joint stock marketing company, controls a larger proportion of exports. The New Zealand Produce Marketing Association, which in 1927 controlled about 10 per cent. of the export, is a purely co-operative organisation with interesting connections with the British consumers' movement.[1] The Co-operative Dairy Company, although its member societies are co-operative, itself approximates in form to a joint-stock company. Private firms in Great Britain maintain direct non-co-operative relations with New Zealand producers. In 1923 a Dairy Produce Export Control Board was established, which is still in operation. In 1927 an experiment in price control was made, but this has been discontinued. The Control Board now confines its operations to general supervision of shipments.

FRUIT.—Fruit (principally apples) is a comparatively small but increasing New Zealand export. A Fruit Export Control Board exists on similar lines to the Dairy Board. The business side of its operations are in the hands of a co-operative organisation, the New Zealand Fruit Growers' Federation, which handles all exports, but of which all producers are not necessarily members. The Control Board has a representative in England who nominates agents for the sale of fruit, a proportion being in this way consigned to the Overseas Farmers' Federations.

WOOL.—The primary marketing of this extremely important commodity is not co-operatively organised, but small quantities are sometimes co-operatively exported.

MEAT, HONEY, AND KAURI GUM.—These three commodities, the first of large and the other two of comparatively small value, are all the subject of Export Control Boards. Meat is not co-operatively handled to any large extent, though a few co-operative meat-freezing companies exist, and certain sales are effected through the New Zealand Produce Marketing Association. A co-operative Honey

[1] See chapter on Joint Undertakings.

Producers' Association exists which handles practically the entire export and works in close collaboration with the Control Board.

SOUTH AFRICA

All co-operative Associations in South Africa which receive the assistance of the State Agricultural Bank are bound to market their produce through co-operative channels. The Federated Farmers' Co-operative Association receives a considerable proportion of various crops, and markets them through the Overseas Farmers' Federations in London.

FRUIT.—(1) *Dried Fruit*—In 1924 the exports were 12,489,447 lbs. (value £214,165), mainly raisins and currants, and represented a large proportion of the total output. The main portion of the export was handled co-operatively.

(2) *Fresh Fruit ; Deciduous and Citrus Fruit*—The fresh fruit exports for 1924 were valued at £439,526. In 1925 70 to 75 per cent. of the lemon growers were co-operatively organised. At present fruit export is concentrated in the hands of the Fruit Growers' Co-operative Citrus and Deciduous Exchange, which handles a very large proportion of the commodity. It is linked with an organisation which undertakes shipping, and with the Overseas Farmers' Federations, who deal with the fruit on its arrival in Europe, generally by allocating it to suitable salesmen. A Perishable Fruit Board also exists, set up by Government, with growers' representatives. The Overseas Farmers' Federations have recently started a system of supplying boxes to growers which are paid for out of the returns on the crop shipped in them.

MAIZE.—The Overseas Farmers' Federations receive a large proportion of the maize crop of Rhodesia, but apparently not that of South Africa, although the latter is the subject of co-operative marketing within the Union.

COTTON.—In 1925 co-operative sales of cotton amounted to 2,724 bales on the home market, and 1,376 bales abroad. The total export of cotton in 1924 was 3,999,388 lbs.

WOOL.—In 1925 the Overseas Farmers' Federations received wool to the value of £29,569, which equalled 8 per cent. of the total wool export of the Union.

TOBACCO.—The bulk of the tobacco crop in South Africa and Rhodesia is co-operatively handled and exported, but not through the Overseas Farmers' Federations. In 1923 the co-operative organisations handled 3,307,807 lbs. of tobacco, and in 1924 they sold 450,000 lbs., or 68 per cent., of the total export.

The other large South African exports, such as *sugar, hides and skins, mohair and feathers*, do not appear to be handled co-operatively to any considerable extent.

IRISH FREE STATE

Irish co-operative marketing is carried out independently of that of any other Dominion. Practically all export is to Great Britain.

BUTTER.—The Irish export of butter in 1927 was as follows:

			Cwt.	£
Creamery	..	..	419,056	3,335,859
Factory	..	..	159,433	1,187,678
Farmers'	..	..	7,012	50,877
			585,501	4,574,414

A large percentage of the butter production of Ireland has for many years been co-operatively organised, and a federation had its own selling agency in London; this had, however, the regular support of only a few societies. In the present year a scheme was adopted to reorganise the industry and its marketing, and give it a completely co-operative character. Government credit was advanced to buy out the remaining proprietary creameries, and a voluntary central marketing organisation, the Irish Associated Creameries, Ltd., was created and began to function in April, 1928. It has secured the adhesion of 88 per cent. of all creameries, handling 70 per cent. of the milk. A small number of co-operative creameries remain outside the organisation and market their produce independently in Great Britain.

BACON AND PORK.—The export of pig products in 1927 was 822,820 cwt., value £3,776,599. A certain number of co-operative bacon factories exist, but it is difficult to say what proportion of this total was handled by them. Probably it was not large.

EGGS.—The export of Irish eggs of all kinds in 1927 was 593,547,840, value £3,039,226. A Government Grading Act is in force and a number of co-operative egg societies are registered as exporters, but their output is not known and probably forms only a small portion of the total. There is a tendency to attach co-operative egg and poultry marketing to the co-operative creameries.

It does not appear that the export of either live-stock or meat is co-operatively handled; neither is the comparatively small trade in liquid milk, cream, and cheese.

PALESTINE

The principal export of Palestine is *oranges*, valued at £435,059 in 1923, the major portion of which is co-operatively marketed.

In 1923–4 over 2,000,000 lbs. of tobacco was produced, of which 538,000 lbs. was co-operatively marketed; but it is uncertain how much was exported.

INDIA

Co-operation in India is principally concerned with credit, and also to a certain extent with the supply of requirements. There are, however, small co-operative sales of *grain* and *jute* and somewhat larger sales of *cotton*, which in 1925 totalled 80,000 bales.

JAMAICA

A co-operative *banana* marketing association was formed in 1927, and is at present handling its first crop. It is not possible to say at present what relation this bears to total production.

WEST AFRICA

Co-operative cocoa marketing organisations exist, but their turnover is unknown.

NEWFOUNDLAND

The marketing of fish is largely on a co-operative basis.

GREAT BRITAIN

Great Britain itself as a co-operative producer will be dealt with at length in succeeding chapters. It may be stated here that only about 2 per cent. or 3 per cent. of the total agricultural production of this country is co-operatively marketed, the proportions for individual commodities being as follows: Live-stock, 3·7 per cent.; dairy produce, 2·5 per cent.; wool, 7 per cent.; poultry and eggs, 3 per cent. The percentage of grain marketed co-operatively is very small, the percentage of fruit probably somewhat larger, but the figures are not ascertainable. In 1927 hops were handled by a co-operative marketing association to the extent of 92 per cent. of the acreage. This is not included in the total given above.

Several countries outside the British Empire are not only exporters of co-operative produce, but send this produce to Great Britain in such quantities that their trade requires to be described in some detail.

DENMARK

BUTTER.—Of the dairies in Denmark, 86 per cent. (handling the milk of 86 per cent. of the dairy cows) are co-operative, and 85 per cent. of the farmers are members of these dairies. From 1906 butter has been exported under a national brand originally instituted by co-operative dairies. The butter exports of Denmark in 1924 reached 123,400 metric tons, which amounted to 38 per cent. of the world export. A very large proportion of this goes to Great Britain. In 1922 there existed eleven co-operative export federations handling 38·8 per cent. of the total export. They were grouped in a price-fixing committee which determined the price in consultation with a similar committee of private dealers.

BACON.—The Danish Bacon exports of 1924 were 197,172 tons, and in the previous year 85 per cent. of the Danish production was sold in Great Britain; forty-nine co-operative slaughterhouses exist, dealing with 82 per cent. of the pigs, with 85 per cent. of the farmers as members. Middlemen have been practically eliminated from the bacon trade; half the co-operative slaughterhouses have agents in England, and the rest deal direct with English retailers. The Danish Co-operative Bacon Trading Company was established in England in 1902. It has eighteen member slaughterhouses, and handles one-third of the Danish bacon sold in England. The Company acts as agent and wholesaler, and charges a commission of $1\frac{1}{4}$ per cent.; net profits are divided between member slaughterhouses and purchasers, whether these are co-operative or not.

EGGS.—The value of eggs exported in 1925 was approximately £6,000,000, of which over 90 per cent. came to Great Britain. A little over 25 per cent. of the total exportation was supplied in the proportion of about three-eighths and five-eighths respectively by seven co-operative slaughterhouses, and by the Central Danish Co-operative Egg Exporting Society.

RUSSIA

The national trade of the U.S.S.R., both internal and foreign, is carried on on three systems, in the following proportions: Private trade, 37 per cent.; co-operative trade, 52 per cent.; state trade, 11 per cent. In recent years co-operative trade has been increasing at the expense of the other two systems. The two main divisions of co-operation in Russia, as in other countries, are consumers' co-operation, with the Centrosojus—a body combining the functions of Union and C.W.S.—at its head, and agricultural co-operation,

centralised in the Selskosojus. Neither of these bodies,
however, confines itself exclusively to production or consumption, nor is there any marked cleavage between industry and agriculture in their composition. Of the fifteen
million members of the co-operative movement, nine millions
are peasants. Of the total peasant population, about
25 per cent. are members of the Centrosojus and 26 per cent.
(in many cases probably the same individuals) are members
of the Selskosojus. The Centrosojus is, however, the
stronger of the two organisations, and a year or two ago was
doing four-fifths of the co-operative trade. Agricultural
co-operation deals with the supply of requirements, credit,
and marketing. Marketing organisation has made the most
progress in recent years. At the same time, Centrosojus
buys very extensively from peasants, as well as peasants'
organisations, and is a large exporter of agricultural produce,
principally grain, but also other raw materials. An attempt
is being made to hand over the export of this produce, and
especially foodstuffs, to the agricultural organisations, but,
owing to various causes—the need of the Centrosojus for
foreign currency to finance its imports, and of good relations
with foreign co-operative societies and the relative weakness
of the agricultural societies in foreign trade—the consumers'
organisations continue to export on a considerable scale.

In 1926 the total membership of agricultural co-operative
societies stood at 7,379,000, drawn especially from dairying,
potato, and tobacco growing districts, and their trade was
as follows:

Agricultural requirements ..   1,049,000,000 roubles.
Agricultural produce   2,003,000,000   ,,

Agricultural marketing by the consumers' organisations reached a value of 599,000,000 roubles.

The following table shows the percentage of the total output of staple products collected respectively by agricultural and consumers' organisations, together with similar percentages referring to exports:

	Percentage of Total Collected.		Percentage of Exports.	
	Agricultural Organisations.	Consumers' Organisations.	Agricultural Organisations.	Consumers' Organisations.
Grain	17	21	6	9
Butter	57	8	66	—
Eggs	30	30	38	12
Flax	34	18	35	11
Wool	45	—	—	—

In the previous year it was calculated that the agricultural co-operative societies also handled 92 per cent. of milk products other than butter; 70 per cent. tobacco; 44 per cent. sugar beet; 76 per cent. of the cotton coming on the market; and a proportion of poultry, honey, potatoes, hides and tar.

The co-operative societies of the U.S.S.R. have foreign depots in England, Germany, France, the Baltic States, the U.S.A., and China.   In 1926, £7,727,568[1] worth of Russian produce was exported through these agencies and £2,861,282[1] of foreign goods imported.   This equalled about 10 per cent. of the total foreign trade of the U.S.S.R.   The co-operative imports are a feature of peculiar interest in the Russian situation, and will be returned to later.   Great Britain was, and is, the largest single participant in the co-operative

[1] Trade has since considerably extended in both directions.

foreign trade of the U.S.S.R. and accounted for 45 per cent. of the turnover—59 per cent. of the exports of raw material, and 28 per cent. of the imports. On the Russian side the trade with Great Britain was divided between Selskosojus (65 per cent.), Centrosojus (28·5 per cent.), the Flax-Growers' Union (2·5 per cent.), and the Ukrainian Union (3 per cent.). Centrosojus was principally engaged in the general import trade, Selskosojus only importing agricultural requirements, mainly machinery. Both exported. The principal exports to London in 1925 were as follows:

Butter	..	..	..	2,100,025
Fibre	..	..	..	675,541
Eggs	..	..	..	731,331

Grain was also a large export, but was sold through the Government grain agency, Exportkhleb, being the subject of a special arrangement, which is in itself an important co-operative development and will be discussed in detail later on. The imports from Great Britain for the same period were given as follows in a recent publication of the Centrosojus:

	£
Colonial and Edible	.. ..	605,983
Textiles	.. ..	463,685
Agricultural machinery	.. ..	122,792
Household goods ..	.. ..	3,242
Haberdashery ..	.. ..	8,880
Instruments ..	.. ..	104,906

These figures give a general indication of the importance of the U.S.S.R. as a co-operative exporter and importer in the last year, for which complete figures are available, and with special reference to the British market. They indicate also the opportunities which exist for inter-trading between the British and Russian co-operative movements. The extent to which these opportunities have been used will be described in a future chapter.

UNITED STATES OF AMERICA

WHEAT.—Wheat Pools exist in the U.S.A., though not on the same scale as in Canada, nor is their crop exported to the same extent. The Pools were started in 1920 and 1921. In 1924, 3,134 elevator associations existed with a membership of 443,000 growers, their combined turnover being about $170,000,000. Pools usually cover a state, but sometimes several states. In 1926 there were ten with a membership of 95,500. In 1924-25 they handled 27,637,000 bushels of grain, or about 3 per cent. of the total output.

WOOL.—In 1923 the total production of wool in the U.S.A. was 266,110,000 lbs., of which 7 per cent. was handled co-operatively.

COTTON.—In 1925-26 the co-operative organisations handled 1,488,000 bales, or 9·3 per cent. of the total cotton production. The Central Co-operative Cotton Association has five agencies abroad, including one at Liverpool.

FRUIT.—The U.S.A. supplies 83 per cent. of the total British imports of dried apricots and prunes. Of the total U.S.A. output in 1922, 26 per cent., value $12,453,726, was marketed co-operatively. In California alone the percentage was as high as 75 to 85 per cent.

In 1926 the " Sunmaid Raisin Company," a co-operative organisation, sold 90 per cent. of the Californian (that is, practically the whole U.S.A.) crop of raisins. The company has recently greatly extended its sales in Canada, Europe, and the Far East.

In 1922; 61 per cent. of the U.S.A. citrus fruit (70 to 75 per cent. of the Californian production, and 35 to 40 per cent. of that of Florida) was marketed co-operatively. It was valued at $69,202,327, and was to the extent of 98 per cent. in the hands of five federations, the largest being the Californian Fruit Growers' Exchange and the Florida Citrus Exchange.

TOBACCO.—Tobacco to the amount of 431,400,233 lbs., or 34 per cent. of the total U.S.A. harvest, is handled by co-operative organisations. In 1924-25 the Burley Tobacco Growers' sold 10,000,000 lbs. on the foreign market, and other associations also export. The co-operative organisation controls 60 per cent. of all Burley tobacco.

MEAT.—No figures are available later than 1919, when co-operative meat societies handled 9,939,512 head of cattle. These appear, however, to have been principally for the home trade.

ALGERIA

In 1925-26, 25 per cent. of the *orange* and *tangerine* crop, amounting to 11,700 tons, was handled by a co-operative association.

The total tobacco production is 660,000 cwt., and is very largely co-operative.

ARGENTINA

Co-operative marketing of *wheat* is beginning, but is not of any considerable extent at present.

BULGARIA

The co-operative production of *tobacco* in 1925 was 15,449,398 lbs. (or nearly 70 per cent. of the total), of which 5,639,581 lbs. or about one-third was exported, principally to places on the Continent.

FINLAND

The export of *butter* from Finland in 1925 was 13,189 tons, of which 92 per cent. was co-operative, 70 to 80 per cent. being from the Central Co-operative Society.

Of *cheese* about 70 per cent. was co-operative.

EGYPT

A few small *cotton*-growing societies exist.

ESTONIA

In 1925, 84 per cent. of the Estonian *butter* production was co-operative, 266 out of the 349 dairies working for export being under co-operative management.

Flax is produced co-operatively to the extent of about 54 per cent. of the total.

In 1923 co-operative organisations exported 1,384,200 *eggs*, or 33 per cent. of the total export.

GREECE

Raisins are marketed co-operatively to a considerable extent, as much as 40 to 65 per cent. in some districts.

HUNGARY

Various agricultural commodities, *wheat, wine, flax*, etc., are marketed co-operatively, but it is difficult to say to what extent produce is exported. In 1926 the *Honey* Co-operatives exported 260 tons, or 63 per cent. of the total.

ITALY

Co-operative societies exist which handle the *lemon* harvest, also *silk* cocoons, but their turnover is not ascertainable.

JAPAN

Silk co-operative societies are in existence, but it is not known whether they export.

LATVIA

In 1925, 90 per cent. of the *butter* and 54 per cent. of the Latvian *cheese* exports were co-operative, also a large proportion of *flax*.

NETHERLANDS

In 1925, 65 per cent. of the output of *butter*, 45 per cent. of the output of *cheese*, and 25 per cent. of the output of *eggs*, was co-operative. Co-operative export societies are in existence.

POLAND

There are considerable co-operative exports of *flax*.

SWEDEN

Certain co-operative exports of *butter* take place, but it is uncertain to what extent.

SWITZERLAND

A considerable proportion of the Swiss production of *cheese* is co-operative, and the co-operative societies have a voice in the control of cheese exportation.

THE CO-OPERATIVE WHOLESALE SOCIETY
AND ITS SUPPLIES

THE Co-operative Wholesale Society is a trading organisation registered under the Industrial and Provident Societies Act. It has a membership of 1,141 registered co-operative societies, and its business is to supply them with goods of every description. Its sales in the year 1927 (fifty-five weeks) amounted to £86,495,960. Its purchases for the same period (including transfers from productive works) amounted to £76,992,053, the difference being accounted for by cost of handling and by the " surplus " which is distributed at the rate of 3d. in the £ on purchases to members, and 1½d. in the £ to non-members. This sum is divided[1] amongst various departments as follows:

Groceries and Provisions	.. ..	65,537,230
Drapery	.. ..	5,400,265
Woollens and ready mades	.. ..	1,788,473
Shoes and Leather ..	.. ..	2,579,909
Coal	.. ..	2,054,477
Furnishings	.. ..	3,563,086
Export	.. ..	300,872
Tea, cocoa, and chocolate	.. ..	6,424,487

Included in the above figures are goods to the value of £28,903,135, derived during the same period from the C.W.S. own productive works. Coal and furnishings may be ruled out of consideration at once as being of no interest to

[1] These figures do not total correctly, as the last item concerns the joint operations of the English and Scottish Co-operative Wholesale Societies.

agriculturists. Drapery, woollens, and shoes and leather are all based on agricultural raw materials, but their value is so largely due to processing that the sums quoted may be taken to represent very little to the agriculturist. In addition it does not appear that any of these departments actually buy to any extent from co-operative sources. The question of wool and leather, however, will be resumed later. Tea, cocoa, and chocolate will also be treated in their place, but though agricultural products, their importance from the co-operative point of view is more potential than actual. The item of present interest to co-operators is the £65,537,230 worth of goods handled by the grocery and provisions department.

In obtaining its supplies the C.W.S. has several methods open to it. It may, and to a very limited extent it does, carry its own production back to its source in the land. It farms some 18,500 acres and supplies itself with produce of various kinds, to the value (in 1927) of £220,520. This, however, represents little over 0·2 per cent. of its total sales; the grain, for instance, according to the C.W.S.'s own statement, would not fill one sack in 600 of those used by the mills. The farms, moreover, are run at a loss, and the considered policy of the C.W.S. is now to carry co-operation on to the land, not by farming itself, but by buying where possible from organised farmers. This does not mean that the existing farms have been abandoned, but rather that they are being used as a check on prices and a test of agricultural conditions in general.

On the other hand, the C.W.S. may buy in the open market through a broker or middleman like any other merchant. It began with this method, but its ideal has always been to get back as close as possible to the sources of production. In pursuit of this ideal it has undertaken one after another of the productive processes and confined its buying more and more to raw materials. It has also attempted to minimise its dealings with middlemen, and where it cannot produce from the source at least to buy from the man who has done so.[1] In some cases it buys agricultural produce straight from the individual farmer, in others from a farmers' co-operative organisation or selling agency. For this purpose it established depots dealing in various commodities in different parts of England and Ireland, also in Copenhagen, Aarhus, Odense, Esbjerg, Jersey, Rouen, Denia, Montreal, New York, Sydney, and several points in West Africa. Before the War the C.W.S. was, with the exception of the Swiss Union, the only co-operative consumers' organisation purchasing from farmers' co-operative societies in another country. Relations existed at first only with Irish and Danish organisations; later, also, with those of Sweden and Holland. After the War trade was opened with co-operative societies in Canada, Australia, and South Africa, and joint agencies set up by the C.W.S. and the farmers' organisations of Russia and New Zealand. Later an International Co-operative Wholesale Society was formed, though it has not so far undertaken actual trading operations. By 1923 it was estimated that the C.W.S. purchases of co-operative origin amounted to £6,509,737, or nearly 10 per

---

[1] A good deal of direct purchase from English farmers took place during the War which was not due principally to policy. Much of this disappeared after the War.

cent. of the total.   By 1926 the total sales of the C.W.S.
were £76,585,764, its imports stood at £28,252,961, of which
£11,420,657, or 40 per cent. of the imports and nearly 15 per
cent. of the total were estimated to be bought from foreign
co-operatives or through depots opened abroad.   Not all
these goods are purchased in the country of origin.   As has
been seen some of the Dominion co-operative organisations
themselves have depots in England, and a large part of their
trade also passes to the C.W.S. through the hands of private
brokers.   It will be useful to consider the principal commodities separately.

GRAIN AND FLOUR.—The C.W.S. has a wheat-buying office
at Liverpool which purchases on the world market.   It also
has a number of mills turning out flour, wheatmeal, and offals
of various types.   It sold in 1927 grain to the value of
£3,900,000, and flour to the value of £8,047,000.   It also
sold 3,446,120 sacks of offals, of which the value is not
specified.[1]   Purchases from the different sources vary from
year to year according to harvests, prices, and other conditions.   In 1925 it was estimated that 55 per cent. of wheat
was from Canada and the U.S.A.   Not more than 10 per cent.
is usually derived from Great Britain itself.

Canada.—The most important co-operative source of
wheat is Canada, where supplies are controlled by the
Canadian Co-operative Wheat Pool.   The C.W.S. sometimes
purchases at its Canadian depot, but more often in England.
A small amount (less than 0·2 per cent.) figures on the C.W.S.
books as bought from the Canadian Co-operative Wheat

[1] In bulk offals and flour represent respectively about 40 per cent.
and 60 per cent. of the total.

Producers, and this may possibly be the extent of direct purchases, but a very much larger amount comes to the C.W.S. through the wheat market in London.   All C.W.S. purchases of Canadian wheat, however, may be taken as co-operative in origin.   The Wheat Pool and the C.W.S. are in fairly close and frequent touch with one another, and in 1927 10 per cent. of the wheat sales in this country went to the C.W.S., but there is no organic connection between them.   At one time some doubts were current in the English co-operative world as to character of the Canadian Pool, which was felt to be monopolistic rather than co-operative.[1] But feeling has recently altered for the better, and representatives of British Industrial Co-operation took part in the International Wheat Pool Conference of 1928.

U.S.S.R.—The next most important source of co-operative wheat is Russia, where all export is conducted through co-operative channels.   Some years ago a joint company was formed, in which the C.W.S. participated with Russian co-operative societies, and which undertook the sale of wheat. This being one of the most interesting developments in co-operative practice, it will be described in the next chapter, together with another experiment of the same type.   At present it is only necessary to say that the C.W.S. obtains considerable supplies in this way.   The formation of the company was at first regarded with some hostility by Canadian co-operators, but Russian and Canadian wheat growers have since met on friendly terms at the International Wheat Pool Conferences.

[1] The consumers' movement of Canada sent a resolution to the International Co-operative Conference at Stockholm in 1927 strongly supporting the Pool.

Australia.—As has been explained in a preceding chapter, the export of Australian wheat is to a considerable extent under co-operative control. For some years past the C.W.S. has financed the movement of the wheat crop by the West Australian Pool, and has been able to do so on terms more favourable to the farmers than those offered by the Australian banks and guaranteed by the State Government. In 1927 a crop of 11,000,000 bushels was financed in this way, and it is expected that in 1928 the sum involved will be about £4,000,000. During one season the C.W.S. also financed the South Australian Pool, but this arrangement was discontinued when similar terms were offered by the Commonwealth Bank. To a certain extent the C.W.S. buys wheat direct from the West Australian Pool, and when it does so it receives the brokerage. The Westralian Farmers have become a member of the C.W.S., and they and other Australian co-operative bodies have been visited by C.W.S. representatives, with a view to establishing good relations.

U.S.A.—This is also a source of C.W.S. wheat, but the States Wheat Pools, which are not strong organisations, are at present selling increasingly on the home market.

Argentina.—The C.W.S. buys largely from the Argentine through agents in that country. A small quantity of grain comes from co-operative societies, though the bulk is from unorganised farmers. It is probable, however, that the next few years will see great development in co-operative marketing in Argentina.

India, Manchuria, Egypt, Chile, also supply small quantities of wheat.

England.—The C.W.S. buys considerably from farmers' co-operative societies as well as from unorganised farmers. This trade will be dealt with in more detail in a later chapter. The C.W.S. has expressed its willingness to buy wheat from co-operative farmers in any part of the Empire, if they will get into direct communication with the Society.

DAIRY PRODUCE: BUTTER, EGGS, AND CHEESE.—The C.W.S. sold in 1927 £8,489,000 worth of butter and £1,508,000 worth of cheese. Its purchases of eggs were between 5¾ and 6 millions, very largely from abroad, and amounted in value to £831,217. The C.W.S. has three butter blending factories, the principal being at Brislington. In 1926 it was doing a trade of 110 to 120 tons a week, and, according to its own statement, had " ample scope to take a considerable amount of farmers' butter, provided they would organise to send larger quantities and improve packing." The C.W.S. depot at Cardiff does, in fact, collect certain quantities of butter from Welsh farmers' societies. The C.W.S. also purchases very largely from abroad, and over 70 per cent. of its total supplies are of co-operative origin.

Denmark.—This country is the C.W.S. largest supplier. The C.W.S. takes nearly one-third of the Danish export of butter, eggs, bacon. While Danish exports to this country have risen by 4 per cent., those to the C.W.S. have risen by 12 per cent. and 20 per cent. of the total butter exports. In 1925, out of 38,100 tons of butter imported by the C.W.S., 24,000 tons (or 63 per cent.) were from Denmark, all or nearly all from co-operative organisations, and to a large extent sold through the Danish Co-operative Wholesale Society. As has been mentioned, the C.W.S. has four depots in the country.

Ireland.—A relatively small quantity of butter (about 1·6 per cent.) comes from Ireland; partly from the C.W.S. own creameries,[1] and partly through the Agricultural Wholesale Society, or from independent co-operative creameries. In future all purchases will be made through the newly formed Irish Associated Creameries. The Irish trade is increasing and is being pushed by the C.W.S. It is to some extent retarded by the fact that winter dairying is not carried on in Ireland. Eggs are also purchased in fairly large quantities from Ireland.

New Zealand.—The C.W.S. and the New Zealand Co-operative Producers have formed a joint company (to be described more fully in the next chapter) for the sale of butter and cheese in this country. From this company the C.W.S. derives 3 or 4 per cent. of its supplies of butter and about 18 per cent. of its supplies of cheese.

Canada.—The C.W.S. takes a proportion of the output of the Quebec Farmers' Federation every year. In one year fairly large purchases of eggs were made from Saskatchewan, but this has not been repeated. Cheese is bought from the Ontario Dairymen's Co-operative Association.

Australia.—Some butter and also eggs are bought through the Overseas Farmers' Co-operative Federations, with whom trade is fairly extensive, though not confined to these commodities.

---

[1] Some time ago the C.W.S. opened a number of creameries in Ireland, with the object of ensuring its butter supplies. In more recent years, and with the growth of an independent farmers' co-operative movement in Ireland, the majority of these creameries have been disposed of, leaving only one central creamery and two auxiliaries in the hands of the C.W.S.

Finland.—The C.W.S. takes all the butter the Finnish co-operative movement can send.

Russia.—There is a trade in butter with the Centrosojus, which in 1925 valued £305,176.

Cheese is also bought from Holland, and eggs from this and other sources.

England.—Besides the butter buying already noted, cheese is bought from farmers' societies in Melton Mowbray, Stilton, Wrexham, and other parts of Derby and Cheshire, also from West Wales and from individual farmers in Somerset. Eggs, both fresh and pickled, are bought from a number of farmers' societies in England and Wales. This trade is small in comparison to C.W.S. total purchases, though not unimportant to the societies concerned.

MILK.—The C.W.S. handled milk to the value of £860,402 in 1927. This business differs from that in other commodities, partly because milk is highly perishable (though hardly less so than green fruit), partly because it is entirely of English origin, and partly because it has to be treated before being passed on to the customer—three conditions which are not found together in the case of any other product. The C.W.S. purchases to a very limited extent from co-operative dairy societies. In these cases the society usually contracts for twelve months in advance at a price based on the N.F.U. agreement with the Federation. The society collects milk from farmer members, cleans, pasteurises, and cools it, and rails it direct to the retail co-operative society. The C.W.S. merely acts as agent. The usual method of the C.W.S., however, is to work through collecting stations of its own. It has eight of these depots in different parts of England (Basford, Bruton, Chargely, Claydon, Congleton, Fole, Melksham, Yulesbury).

The Claydon depot may be taken as an example. It handles about 60,000 gallons per week, collecting in its own lorries from farmers, pasteurising and cleaning and dispatching to retail societies all over the Eastern Counties and in London. One morning's milk is distributed to customers on the following morning. For one society, which has its own pasteurising plant, the C.W.S. merely acts as agent, the milk itself going straight from the farmers to the society. In all cases the C.W.S. enters into a contract with retail societies for a fixed supply of milk, except in that of societies just entering the milk business, to whom they supply as required from week to week. Prices to the farmer are fixed by the joint N.F.U. and Wholesalers' Committee; the C.W.S. also offers an alternative contract, differing slightly in conditions, though not in price, which is generally accepted by the farmers. The C.W.S. inspects farms and tests milk for cleanliness and butter-fat content.

The depot also acts as an agency through which the C.W.S. buys wheat, seeds, etc., from the farmers, and sells feeding stuffs, offals, cake, etc. This counter trade represents in value about 10 per cent. of the milk trade. Some payments are in cash, some are offset against milk deliveries.

MEAT, PORK, BACON.—About £1,024,126 of *meat* passes through the hands of the C.W.S., of which 66 per cent. is imported, a large proportion coming through the C.W.S. agents in the Argentine. The proportion of C.W.S. imported to home-killed meat is very much larger than the proportion actually consumed by members of co-operative societies, as nearly all meat imports pass through the hands of the C.W.S., while the retail societies buy a large amount of their home-killed meat independently from farmers or on local markets. A small proportion of Argentine meat, and some from New Zealand, is of co-operative origin. A joint company similar to that which handles butter and cheese is now being formed with New Zealand producers. Meat is amongst the commodities which the C.W.S. is ready to buy, either from individual farmers or co-operative societies, but it would appear that the trade is comparatively small.

In 1927 the C.W.S. handled *bacon* to the value of £4,880,000. It has bacon factories of its own in England, Ireland, and Denmark, with products worth £928,567. The bulk of its supplies were imported, to a very great extent, from Denmark, over three-fifths through the C.W.S. branches in that and other countries. Supplies to the value of £354,122 come from the Co-operative Bacon Trading Company, and all bacon is probably in some measure co-operatively handled on the Danish side. The company pays a dividend on business done to all suppliers and also to retailers, whether co-operative or not, in which the C.W.S. participates. Ireland and the U.S.A. are also sources of C.W.S. bacon. Purchases were made from a farmers' organisation in South Africa, and a small quantity is purchased in England.

FRUIT.—In 1927 green fruit was sold to the value of £1,266,000, besides dried and bottled fruit and vegetables. About 20 per cent. of canned and dried fruit is from the British Empire. The C.W.S. buys both on the home and foreign markets. It makes considerable purchases direct from the source, but these vary in accordance with seasons, requirements, etc. Purchases are also made at markets, and the C.W.S. has an office at Covent Garden. It buys to a relatively small extent from farmers' co-operative societies and auction marts. Where, however, the C.W.S. has been in the habit of buying from individual farmers, and a co-operative society is subsequently formed, the C.W.S. frequently continues to buy from the farmer direct. A good deal of fruit is also sold on commission by the C.W.S. for various individual and co-operative growers. In so doing the C.W.S. assumes something like the position of a co-operative marketing organisation for the farmer, but one in which he has no membership or vote. The C.W.S. prefers graded produce, but takes only first grade fruit, and farmers frequently find it difficult to dispose of the second grade. The C.W.S. is also anxious to see the use of non-returnable empties. About one million hundredweight of potatoes are handled yearly at ten different depots in the growing districts; 98 per cent. of these potatoes are bought direct from the growers, a little from farmers' societies. Seed potatoes are sold extensively to English and Scottish societies.

The C.W.S. has jam and pickle factories which turned out goods, value £1,616,833 in 1927. Fruit for jam is mostly bought in bulk and separately from the ordinary fruit purchases. About 6,000 tons is required yearly.

The C.W.S. has a depot in Jersey principally for the purchase of tomatoes and early potatoes. Produce is always sold " on the bridge," a sort of open-air market at which the sales are really by private treaty, but in competition with other farmers. The farmers consider they are exploited by rings, and there have been recent and not apparently very successful attempts at price-fixing.

The C.W.S. also has a depot at Denia in Spain, and both oranges and raisins are purchased from this country. The C.W.S. has been in the habit of buying outright, as near the source of production as possible, and dispatching to England. No farmers' co-operative societies are known. Relations with the farmers are harmonious, and the latter frequently leave payments to accumulate in the hands of the C.W.S. During 1927 the Spanish Government set up an export control board which registers all foreign sales, and fixes prices for the different grades. It further limits the amount which may be sold on commission. A very high price was secured at first, followed by a slump.

The C.W.S. also purchases raisins to a large extent in *Greece*, one of its representatives travelling there for the purpose. The method is to advance up to 85 per cent. of the price. Greece has also a government control board which works well. It buys up a portion of the raisin crop each year, and only releases it by degrees and as seems desirable.

Canada and the U.S.A.—The C.W.S. buys direct from growers' organisations in these countries, including raisins, citrus, and hard fruits. Oranges are bought from *South Africa*, direct from growers. Trade with *New Zealand and Australia* has not been developed at present. Trade is opening with the co-operative societies of the Ukraine, but has not yet reached any considerable proportions.

MARGARINE.—In 1927 the C.W.S. dealt in margarine to the value of £1,326,786. The materials for this product were largely derived from the C.W.S. depots in Sierra Leone and Nigeria,[1] not of course from any form of farmers' co-operative organisation. The C.W.S. also manufactures *lard* to the value of £1,603,366, and *soap* to the value of £2,705,668. It purchases tallow through its depot in Sydney, but it is doubtful whether any of this is from co-operative sources.

TEA, COFFEE, AND COCOA.—The English and Scottish Co-operative Wholesales have formed a joint society to handle tea, coffee, and cocoa. Tea to the value of £5,926,629 passed through their hands in 1927. A portion of this was produced on the Society's own estates, which comprise 35,574 acres in Ceylon, South India, and Assam, and supply goods to the value of £110,000. The remainder is bought from private merchants in the ordinary way. It has a depot in Ceylon which handles tea and rice. The value of coffee amounted to £347,694, and that of cocoa (derived from the Gold Coast depot) to £577,644.

TOBACCO.—The C.W.S. has its own factory and sells £1,457,253 worth of tobacco. It purchases a small proportion direct from tobacco growers' co-operative societies in the U.S.A.

TEXTILES: CLOTHING, WOOL, LEATHER, ROPE.—The C.W.S. does a very large businses in clothing and leather goods, principally boots and shoes. The value of these depends to a considerable extent on manufacture, and it is difficult to estimate what it represents to the farmer. It is of some

---

[1] The value of supplies (mainly palm kernels) from these depots, together with those from the Gold Coast (which produces cocoa), were £244,643 in 1927.

help to note that while the total value of leather goods is £2,713,154, the value of goods handled by fell-mongeries is £885,987. The value of the produce of woollen mills as distinct from clothing factories is £507,139. About 35 per cent. of this is the product of a mill at Buckfastleigh in Devon. It makes mainly fine serges and consequently imports a large proportion of the wool required from Australia, but it is impossible to say if this is co-operative. About 2,000 fleeces are obtained from a co-operative society in Ireland. The mills also buy fleeces locally, but as the South Devon Wool is of coarse quality, it is mostly forwarded to the C.W.S. mills in the north for use in carpet-weaving, etc. From 1,000 to 2,000 fleeces are bought annually from the North Devon Farmers' Society, and purchases are also made from the Cornwall Farmers. A certain number of skins are bought and made into rugs if of sufficiently good quality. Otherwise the wool is stripped. The C.W.S. also has a fell-mongery at Buckfastleigh, which buys fells direct from the West Devon and North Cornwall Farmers' Slaughter House. Both wool and fells are also bought by the C.W.S. from unorganised farmers. The C.W.S. has a rope and twine works, turning out goods to the value of £97,270.

This practically completes the survey of C.W.S. activities which are of interest to the agricultural producer. It is not easy to estimate with precision the extent to which C.W.S. supplies are co-operative from their origin, or whether the 15 per cent. purchases of co-operative origin have increased or diminished since 1926. Probably outside the purchases from the Anglo-Russian Grain Company, the New Zealand Produce Association, the Overseas Farmers' Federations, the Irish Associated Creameries, and the Danish butter and bacon exporting organisations, the amount of direct trading with farmers' co-operative societies is relatively small, and is confined to limited transactions with local farmers' societies in Great Britain, Ireland, Canada, and the U.S.A. The whole of this direct trade forms an inconsiderable proportion of the C.W.S. total business. On the other hand, a very large proportion of the C.W.S. principal commodities, such as grain, are purchased from the Canadian Wheat Pool and other bodies, through intermediaries, or in some way which does not enable them to figure as complete co-operative purchases. The same could probably be said of supplies from Holland and possibly other Dominions besides Canada. Milk, on the other hand, is scarcely purchased at all from organised farmers, though from the point of view of economies of handling, the C.W.S. system can be open to little objection. Meat and fruit, it would seem, are only derived to a limited extent from co-operative sources, a little in Great Britain and (in the case of fruit) rather more in Canada and the U.S.A. Much the same might be said of wool and leather. The tropical products—tea, cocoa, coffee, rice, sugar, palm kernels, etc.—cannot be described as being co-operative at all, except where their entire production is in the hands of the C.W.S.

Where the co-operative marketing of any commodity has been well organised, as in the case of wheat or butter, there the C.W.S. buys heavily from co-operative sources. Where this is not so, as in the case of tropical products, the C.W.S. has pushed back to the source of production along its own lines. In a few cases, such as that of wool, the fact that the C.W.S. is not a particularly large buyer may have retarded the development of an organised co-operative trade, but it is clear that in nearly every instance the deciding factor has been the attitude and methods of the farmer.

The relations of the C.W.S. with farmers' co-operative organisations is not entirely limited to purchases by the C.W.S. from the farmers. In the following chapters reciprocal trade with the co-operative federations of Russia and New Zealand will be discussed, as well as the C.W.S. sales to farmers' societies in Great Britain. Before going on to these specialised undertakings, however, it may be as well to mention the miscellaneous exports of the C.W.S. to other agricultural countries and organisations.

The exports of the C.W.S. ranking next in importance are those to the Irish Agricultural Wholesale Society which very greatly exceed the sales effected by that body to the C.W.S. These consist on the agricultural side of feeding stuffs— *i.e.*, cotton-seed, meal, feeding cakes, etc., but not of seeds[1] or manures, but they also include a fairly large amount of groceries. The I.A.W.S. is a member of the C.W.S., and recently, in passing through a period of some difficulty, it has received the assistance and financial support of the C.W.S. on lines which will be described in more detail in dealing with some of the English Agricultural Societies.[2]

Fairly large exports also go through the Overseas Farmers' Co-operative Federations; they consist chiefly of clothing

---

[1] The I.A.W.S. buys root seeds from the Eastern Counties Farmers' Association at Ipswich, and in return supplies ryegrass seed obtained from the north of Ireland.

[2] See chapters on The C.W.S. and the Farmers' Societies.

and other domestic goods, including canned goods, principally intended for New Zealand, where the farmers' co-operative organisations have opened retail stores.   Certain shipments of agricultural requirements also take place.

The C.W.S. is in touch with the Canadian retail co-operative societies which have a large agricultural membership, but its sales to them are not at present considerable. The principal Argentine society is a member of the C.W.S., and draws supplies from it.   Small quantities of wheat offals go to Denmark.   The C.W.S. also acts as an agent for the Co-operative Unions of Finland, Estonia, and Iceland, for articles such as dried fruit and sugar.

JOINT UNDERTAKINGS: NEW ZEALAND; RUSSIA

In two cases the C.W.S. has entered into joint marketing organisations with farmers' co-operative marketing associations in other countries. One is with New Zealand, and the other with Russian exporting societies.

New Zealand Produce Association, Ltd.—This company was formed in 1920 by the C.W.S. and the New Zealand Producers' Co-operative Marketing Association. The Marketing Association is a Co-operative Federation, with a membership of ninety-one co-operative dairy factories. Of these factories seventy market cheese and forty-nine butter. The Marketing Association handled about 10 per cent. of the total New Zealand export of butter and cheese. The member societies are not bound to sell through it, nor are their members bound to sell through the societies, as no contracts are in force. In the case of cheese, the fact that there is only one factory to each district usually compels the farmers to send to it; but in the case of butter, farmers now separate milk on their own farms, the local creamery is superseded, and farmers rail their cream to considerable distances if they consider it more advantageous to do so.

The capital of the New Zealand Producers was contributed equally by the C.W.S. and the New Zealand Producers' Co-operative Marketing Association, and consists of a nominal capital of £10,000 and an issued capital of £5,000. The organisation, however, works mainly on bank overdrafts which are required to pay for large shipments as they arrive, but which are paid off by the end of the year. For this purpose the association draws upon the C.W.S. bank.

The company has warehouses in London where produce is stored pending sale; it also has five branches through the country, including some at the ports which handle shipments not coming through London. The commodities dealt in are butter and cheese obtained from member societies in New Zealand. There has also been established a frozen meat department. These commodities are offered for sale in the open market. If the C.W.S. butter and cheese buyer chooses o purchase at the current price, he does so, but the C.W.S. is not compelled to buy, nor the Association to sell; the C.W.S. would probably always buy rather than see the company left with supplies on its hands. When the company was formed, it was hoped to sell the bulk of the produce immediately on arrival to the C.W.S., and for some time the C.W.S. followed the custom of buying in bulk as soon as shipments arrived. It was found, however, that this system was not entirely satisfactory. The C.W.S., therefore, adopted the plan of only buying day to day requirements. This made it necessary for the Association to seek customers on the open market, and to institute a much more elaborate and costly selling agency than was originally intended. The patronage of the C.W.S., however, gave the company breathing-space in which to improvise machinery and secure an alternative outlet. The proportion of C.W.S. to other sales is shown in the following table:

TONNAGE OF SALES. NEW ZEALAND PRODUCE

Year.	Cheese.	Butter.	Percentage of C.W.S. to Total Sales.	
			Cheese. Per Cent.	Butter. Per Cent.
1921	6,380	—	60	—
1922	5,726	2,219	46	37
1923	5,652	2,440	38	18
1924	6,895	1,792	38	19
1925	4,133	2,993	60	16
1926	7,525	2,203	42	38
1927	6,365	2,675	58	28

The percentage of butter bought by the C.W.S. in 1926-1927 was probably higher than it would otherwise have been, owing to the fact that the New Zealand Butter Control was in operation in that year and was carrying out a policy of price-fixing which made it a matter of indifference to the C.W.S. from whom they bought their New Zealand butter, and they therefore bought largely from the New Zealand Producers. No sales are made to retail co-operative societies in membership with the C.W.S. Some sales, however, are made to the Scottish Co-operative Wholesale Society, particularly from shipments arriving in Glasgow.

The company is controlled by two directors appointed by the C.W.S. and two by the New Zealand Produce Association, with a chairman appointed alternatively from each side. The current ruling commission is charged on all sales. All profits, after payment to reserve, etc., are divided equally between the two organisations. The portion going to the C.W.S. is ultimately spread out amongst the retail societies purchasing from it, in proportion to their purchases, and through them to the individual consumer. On the New Zealand side profits are paid over to the Producers Co-operative Marketing Association, which remits them to shippers in proportion to their shipments.

The company also acts as agent for the National Dairy Association of New Zealand, a co-operative supply association covering most of the co-operative dairy factories in New Zealand—many more, that is, than are members of the Producers' Association. The company's functions in this respect are not, however, of a specially co-operative character. They simply ship machinery, parchment, salt, and other dairying requirements, many of them from the Continent rather than England, to New Zealand, and charge a commission for their services. They also ship tea from the C.W.S. depot at Colombo to New Zealand on the same terms.

The commercial relations existing between the co-operative organisations of Great Britain and Russia are of considerable interest and growing importance. They concern both import and export, and cover a number of commodities, not all sold on the same system. The most interesting development is the Anglo-Russian Grain Company, Ltd., which resembles in many ways the New Zealand Producers, Ltd.

The export of grain in Russia has been for some years the monopoly of a limited company, Exportkhleb (Grain export). The shareholders in this company are Centrosojus, Selsko-sojus,[1] the Government grain collecting agencies, and the State Bank. Grain is collected locally by co-operative organisations and Government agencies. In districts where there is a surplus over local requirements, it is forwarded to regional Unions or to the Central Union, for transference to

[1] See p. 47.

areas where local supplies are insufficient. What remains after national requirements have been met is dispatched to the ports for export through the agency of Exportkhleb. In the present year (1928) the bodies forming this organisation have undergone a closer amalgamation, and have been reconstituted as Sojuskhleb (Grain Union). The Exportkhleb has offices in Berlin, Hamburg, Paris, Rotterdam, Geneva, etc. In all these places it sells to consumers' co-operative organisations, and the trade is growing.

The Russo-British Grain Export Company was formed in November, 1923, with a capital of £200,000. Shares are held half by the Exportkhleb, one-quarter by the English Co-operative Wholesale Society, Ltd., and one-quarter by a shipping firm and a firm of grain brokers. The company is governed by a Board of Directors representing the participating organisations in proportion to their shares. The large working capital necessary for the company's operations is borrowed from the Co-operative Wholesale Society's Bank.

The company handles cereals, Soya beans, oil-seeds and oil-cake, manufactured by the co-operative organisations in Russia. The bulk of the grain and seeds is co-operative in origin, except the Soya beans, which are produced in Manchuria. The company purchases grain in bond in Russian ports or in cargo and sells it on a commission basis, mainly in Great Britain, but also to a lesser extent in France, Italy, and South Europe. The professional services of the firms of brokers and shipping agents who are members of the company are utilised in handling the grain and are remunerated in the usual way. The Co-operative Wholesale

Society has the first offer of all grain as it comes on the market at the market price. The total sales and sales to the C.W.S. may be compared in the following table:

SALES OF GRAIN AND SEEDS BY ANGLO-RUSSIAN GRAIN COMPANY.

	Total Sales In Tons.	Sales to C.W.S.	
		In Tons.	Per Cent.
1923–24	259,793	14,276,	5·4
1924–25	119,394	—	—
1925–26	492,873	72,818	14·6
1926–27	421,261	83,029	20

It will be seen that the percentage going to the C.W.S. is a comparatively small one, but that it has grown steadily. Complete figures for the year 1927-28 are not available, but it is said that the sales of the company for this period approach £12,000,000 in value. As a member of the company the C.W.S. gets a rebate on its purchases. All profits, however, are divided according to shares, and, there is no co-operative disposal of surplus. The company has worked well, and was described recently by a director of the C.W.S. as " a nearly perfect system of inter-trading."[1]

Co-operative trade with Russia is by no means limited to grain. Both Centrosojus and Selskosojus have branches in London for the sale of butter, eggs, cheese, bacon, poultry, fruit, flax, hemp, tow, bristles, horsehair, furs, hides and skins, and the purchase of domestic and agricultural requirements. The Moscow Narodny Bank exists to finance co-operative imports and exports; 18 per cent. of its capital is held by agricultural co-operative societies. It carries

[1] A somewhat similar Austro-Russian company, the Ratao, exists in Vienna, importing wheat and eggs from Russia and exporting Austrian manufactured articles.

on credit operations with the assistance of foreign banks—where possible co-operative banks. In 1927 it obtained credits from the co-operative banks of England, France, Germany, Switzerland and Belgium, and the Labour Banks of the U.S.A. to the value of £1,882,585. It also did business with the Co-operative Bank of Palestine. The Moscow Narodny Bank has a branch in London which, besides financing co-operative imports and exports, advances money to cover the cost of collecting raw materials, moving crops, etc. The Bank has credit up to £160,000 from the C.W.S. Bank, £30,000 of which is employed for discounting bills to co-operative centres, and the remainder as revolving credits.

Sales from Centrosojus and Selskosojus to the English and Scottish C.W.S. were at first principally of butter. Trade began in 1922. In 1924 the C.W.S. purchased 25,000 casks of butter valued at £205,162 from the Centrosojus; in 1925, 41,914 casks at £355,176 from Selskosojus, which had now taken over the butter export trade. This amount was equal to 15 per cent. of the total butter sales of the Selskosojus. Recently bacon and other goods began to figure in the purchases of the C.W.S. Sales to the C.W.S. and S.C.W.S., exclusive of grain, together with the percentage of total sales which these represent, stand as follows:

1923	1924	1925	1926	1927	Total.
£1,641	£215,131	£385,107	£310,199	£337,396	£1,249,474
Per cent.	Per cent.	Per cent.	Per cent.	Per cent.	Per cent.
·1	7	8	9	8·4	7·4

It will be observed that the percentage is not a high one, probably owing largely to the fact that fibres, furs, etc.

are not in large demand in the British co-operative movement, so that the staple purchase has tended to be limited
to butter.

At the same time, an almost equally large trade has
passed from the British to the Russian co-operative organisations. The C.W.S. acts as an agent for the Russian societies,
and the Centrosojus purchases (generally on commission) all
the foreign goods required by its member societies. The
Selskosojus also purchases agricultural requirements, chiefly
machinery and implements, but these, except binder-twine,
are not as a rule obtainable from the C.W.S. Purchases
since the trade began are as follows:

	1922	1923	1924	1925	1926	1927	*Total.*
	£	£	£	£	£	£	£
Centro-sojus	28,602	28,796	196,308	360,372	335,978	1,225,959	2,196,015
Selsko-sojus	—	—	—	—	44,483	54,085	98,568
Ukrainian Co-ops.	—	—	17,800	46,400	10,517	8,737	83,454
	28,602	28,796	214,108	406,772	390,978	1,288,781	2,377,037

The purchases of the Centrosojus being of a domestic
character are of less agricultural interest, but in view of its
rural membership they are perhaps worth describing in some
detail. It may be mentioned that this trade would probably
have extended more rapidly than it has done if the Government had not partially restricted the use of credits to the
importation of machinery and similar requirements. The
largest single product purchased by the Centrosojus from
the C.W.S. is tea. The Government Tea Trust—a monopoly
—was put into the hands of the Centrosojus in 1927, and
nearly all its supplies are drawn from the C.W.S., which
allows a permanent credit of £500,000 to £600,000. The

only tea bought elsewhere is a certain proportion coming from China. The complete figures (in sterling) for trade with the C.W.S. are as follows:

	1922	1923	1924	1925	1926	1927	Total.
Herrings	28,602	28,796	171,976	76,604	124,059	210,091	640,128
Tea ..	—	—	24,332	61,034	201,795	957,990	1,245,151
Spices ..	—	—	—	51,142	2,571	25,188	78,901
Coffee, cocoa ..	—	—	—	1,052	2,852	4,768	8,672
Rice ..	—	—	—	82,638	—	—	82,638
Textiles ..	—	—	—	85,907	4,701	—	90,608
Copra ..	—	—	—	—	—	23,573	23,573
Various ..	—	—	—	1,995	—	4,349	6,344
Total	28,602	28,796	196,372	360,372	355,978	1,225,959	2,176,015
Percentage of co-operative purchases of Centrosojus			32·8	31·63	76·97	54·73	49·26

It will be seen that not only is the C.W.S. probably the largest single British supplier of the Centrosojus, but the Centrosojus is also amongst the largest customers of the C.W.S., its purchases in 1927 being about half those of the Scottish Co-operative Wholesale Society, and larger than those of any but the strongest local societies in England. This is largely accounted for by the item of tea.

Comparing the Russian with the New Zealand undertakings, it may be stated briefly that the Russian is more extensive and varied, but that the joint machinery of the Anglo-Russian Grain Company is not itself founded on co-operative principles, while that of the New Zealand Producers is. In the Russian case, on the other hand, counter-trade is more highly developed, and is a sale in the main of genuinely co-operative goods, while such as exists in the case of New Zealand is simply an agency business. Neither the Centrosojus nor the Selskosojus, however, are members of the C.W.S., and they do not therefore receive

6

full dividend on their purchases. These two joint organisations may not represent a complete solution of the problem of linking co-operative production and consumption, but they are the most efficient machinery which has so far been devised to deal with it, and they have been tested by a number of years working. They are the fruit of expert thought and experience, and for all these reasons deserve serious study.

THE FARMERS' SOCIETIES AND THE C.W.S.

THE industrial co-operative movements of England and Wales are merged in one another, and the C.W.S. stands, commercially, at the head of both. The agricultural movements, on the other hand, not only are grouped round separate centres—the National Farmers' Union (which succeeded the Agricultural Organisation Society as the guardian of the agricultural co-operative movement), and the Welsh Agricultural Organisation Society—but they show distinct differences in their character, due to geography and, perhaps, also to race, and to the fact that the W.A.O.S. continued to flourish after the A.O.S. collapsed. They will therefore be treated as two separate groups in the course of this chapter.

There are in England about 400[1] agricultural co-operative societies. Some of these are mainly concerned with the purchase of agricultural requirements—principally feeding stuffs and fertilisers—on behalf of their own members. The chief object of others is the sale of their own members' produce to the public. Several combine both activities, though generally one predominates. Of these societies 200 or more are smallholding or allotment societies, or of some similar type; their principal concern is not as a rule with buying and selling, and only in a few cases do their trading activities

[1] The number is uncertain owing to the societies occupying a border line position which may or may not be included in any given list of agricultural societies.

reach any considerable scale. They do not usually have any connection with the industrial co-operative movement, though there are exceptions.

The total sales of requirements by English agricultural co-operative societies in 1926 was £5,655,093. Of this sum the smallholders societies did not, at the most generous estimate, account for more than £200,000. The societies' sales of agricultural produce for the same year reached the value of £5,420,533, from which about £22,000 should be deducted for the smallholders organisations.

As far as can be estimated there are, not counting the smallholders, 190 farmers' co-operative societies in various stages of growth (and sometimes of decay) with annual sales varying between a few hundred and half a million pounds. There are 111 general trading societies, 51 dairies, 15 egg societies, and 13 fruit societies. In 1926 they sold agricultural requirements to the value of £5,455,093, and agricultural produce to the following values:

			£
Milk and dairy produce	..	..	1,170,050
Eggs and poultry	..	..	334,570
Live stock	..	..	2,693,949
Dead meat	..	..	827,098
Fruit and market garden produce		..	59,896
Sundries (wool, grain, etc.)[1]	..	..	323,910
		Total ..	5,398,533

It should be borne in mind that there are, not included in these figures, a certain number of organisations not regis-

[1] This figure does not appear large enough to include all grain sales, but otherwise their absence from the above figures (drawn from the Report of the Registrar of Friendly Societies) is difficult to explain; probably they are counted as requirements even when they are definitely marketed.

tered under the Industrial and Provident Societies Acts, which are, for all practical purposes, farmers' co-operative societies.

In Wales, in the same year, there were ninety-two societies selling requisites to the value of £1,114,084, and produce to the following values:

	£
Milk and dairy produce	97,025
Eggs and poultry	25,261
Livestock	4,386
Dead meat	20
Fruit and market garden produce ..	303
Sundries	135
Total ..	127,120

These figures and the commodities they represent may now be placed side by side with the sales of the industrial movement for the same year which amounted to £184,879,902. It will be seen that the agricultural sales, even if entirely absorbed by the industrial movement, could not have satisfied more than 3 per cent. of its requirements. It remains to be discovered how much even this 3 per cent. was actually absorbed, and how far the £6,000,000 odd of agricultural requirements were derived from industrial co-operative sources.

As has been seen, the C.W.S. is a large buyer of agricultural produce, and it claims to purchase, at a rough estimate, about £1,000,000 worth of these goods from agricultural co-operative societies. These purchases consist of fruit (a fairly large item), grain (also large and important because widespread), dairy produce (principally milk and cheese), with smaller amounts of fat stock and eggs. The retail societies have

similar direct dealings with farmers' societies, but these will
be more particularly discussed in another chapter.

The C.W.S. is also a very large industrial producer. It
is said to be the largest flour miller in the country; it also
runs oilseed mills and slaughter-houses, and the by-products
of these and other works form the basis of the more important agricultural requirements, principally feeding stuffs.
The C.W.S. has always had a certain market for these commodities amongst the retail industrial societies who have
farms, fatten stock for butchery, sell poultry food to their
members, or (before the use of motors) merely kept vans
and horses for delivery purposes. This, however, has been
insufficient as an outlet for the enormous quantities of
millers' offals and other goods which pour out yearly from
the C.W.S. mills. In 1915 an agricultural department was
created with the object of finding a market for these goods
amongst farmers, and especially amongst organised farmers.
At that time the C.W.S. was already selling about 1,500 tons
of manure and the same amount of feeding cake. In 1916 a
seed department was added and land taken at Derby where
the C.W.S. seeds are grown. It does not buy seeds to any
extent from farmers, except oats from Scotland. The
African Oil Mill, producing oil cake, was purchased in the
same year. A bone-crushing mill was also started.

In 1927 this department of the C.W.S. sold about £1,500,000
worth of goods. Feeding stuffs represent about £1,200,000[1]
(including 50,000 tons of feeding cake), manures about

[1] This, however, is considerably less than the C.W.S. total output
of feeding stuffs, as shown by the following figures: offals (1927)
3,446,120 sacks; feeding cake value £309,000; oil cake £937,329.

£40,000 (40,000 tons), of which £38,000 goes to agricultural societies. The remaining £260,000 represents seeds, paint (from the C.W.S. paint works), small quantities of agricultural hardware, and a little machinery. Further, the C.W.S. has, of recent years, extended to farmers' societies many of the services which it has always been prepared to render to its industrial members. Membership of the C.W.S. has all along been open to farmers' societies, and carries with it a dividend (or bonus) on all purchases from the C.W.S. The Co-operative Insurance Society, which is closely linked with the C.W.S., accepts farmers' insurance, and a number of agricultural societies have become its agents. In 1926 the insurance premiums paid by farmers to the C.W.S. amounted to £50,000, and by farmers' organisations to £20,000. The C.W.S. also placed the resources of its Bank at the disposal of the farmers, and many of them have availed themselves of its services.

After the liquidation of the Agricultural Wholesale Society, a number of agricultural co-operative societies found themselves burdened with crushing liabilities, and one or two, although their membership and turnover were in no way unsatisfactory, were on the verge of liquidation. In several cases, especially in the South-West of England, the C.W.S. offered its collaboration in restoring the society to solvency, and the offer was accepted. In some cases the C.W.S. merely gives generous trading credits, and leaves the society to obtain bank credit through one of the joint stock banks. In others the C.W.S. itself gives bank credits. It is usual in all these cases for the C.W.S. to obtain certain rights of inspection of the society's accounts, which are frequently audited by an official of the C.W.S. auditing department. Sometimes, where the C.W.S. commitments are heaviest, a further step is taken and the C.W.S. appoints a representative to attend the meetings of the society's board of management. This arrangement has obtained for many years in the case of industrial societies which have got into financial difficulties and have been piloted to safety under a measure of C.W.S. control. The C.W.S. has further appointed an official who has his headquarters in the West of England, and whose business it is to advise the agricultural co-operative societies in membership with the C.W.S. This collaboration appears to have been of mutual advantage in every case. The societies themselves are prosperous, the arrangement is popular with them, and they regard the C.W.S. with the same kind of loyalty with which it has always been regarded by the industrial societies.

The closeness of this connection is exceptional, but nearly half the existing agricultural societies are members of the C.W.S., and nearly 70 per cent. (166 societies in England and Wales) have dealings with it, which range from simple inter-trading on a large scale but implying no measure of control, through commercial relations of varying degrees of cordiality, to downright hostility on the part of a farmers' society which still finds it profitable to trade with the C.W.S.

No attempt has hitherto been made to record this trade, to estimate its nature or the place it takes in the turnover of the various societies. In order to secure some data a questionnaire was sent out at the end of 1927 to the 190 farmers' co-operative societies in England, as well as to those in Wales.[1]   Of English societies ninety-one, or nearly half, sent in replies.   They include a large proportion of fruit societies, only two egg societies, and about half the dairies and general trading societies.   Of those replying eight reported that they had ceased business, and twenty-four returned blanks or negatives to every question, nine of these being general societies, three fruit, and twelve dairy. As the total of dairy societies is about half that of general societies, this may be taken as an indication that the dairy societies, which are amongst the largest sellers of produce, are not most numerous amongst those trading with the C.W.S.   It is possible also, for reasons to be considered later, that the egg societies are in the same position.   Finally, sixty-three societies, including forty-five general societies, thirteen dairies, four fruit, and two egg societies, reported transactions with the industrial movement, which in nearly every case appears to mean the C.W.S. for at least a portion of the business recorded.   Those dealing with the C.W.S., therefore, amounted to 69 per cent.; it has been assumed, and the assumption is closely borne out by other evidence, that this proportion is maintained among the societies which failed to reply.   Besides these societies, one replied which omitted to give its name, and three answers came from fruit marts which do not record the produce passing through their hands in such a way as to make it comparable with the sales of other societies.   These societies have, therefore, been excluded from all calculations, except where they are specially mentioned.

[1] The smallholders' societies were also approached, but failed to reply.

The total sales of agricultural requirements by farmers'
co-operative societies to their members in 1926 was, as has
been noted, £5,501,327. The total for the societies from
whom particulars have been obtained is £3,100,110, or
58 per cent.[1] It will thus be observed that 58 per cent. of
the total trade was done by 48 per cent. of the societies.
Of this £3,100,110 worth of agricultural requirements,
£820,760 worth or 26 per cent. was purchased from the
C.W.S. Thus, though 69 per cent. of the societies dealt
with the C.W.S., it was only to the extent of 26 per cent. of
their turnover. This is explained in various ways. For
one thing half a dozen societies only sold their members'
produce to the C.W.S., but did not purchase requirements
form it, at least not in the year under discussion. One
society bought a relatively small quantity (£500) of bran
and middlings from a retail co-operative instead of direct
form the C.W.S. Broadly speaking, however, the percentages indicate, what is actually the fact, that though a
large number of societies deal with the C.W.S., comparatively few deal with it exclusively or even for the major
portion of their supplies. This is even the case with societies
which are on excellent terms with the C.W.S.

Of the 46 societies purchasing from the C.W.S., 38 were
general societies, 4 dairy, 3 fruit, and 1 egg. Their purchases consisted of feeding stuffs, largely millers' offals,

---

[1] There is an element of uncertainty in many of these calculations,
owing to the fact that figures for total trade are all for 1926, and
figures for C.W.S. trade are in some cases for 1927. The discrepancy
is probably not great, but its extent and incidence cannot be known
until another year's figures have been published by the Registrar
of Friendly Societies.

bran, middlings, sharps, also compounds, cotton cake and linseed; grain, imported maize and barley, seeds, seed potatoes, grass and root seeds; fertilisers and artificial manures, slag and supers; oil, petrol, and motor spares; implements and coal. Four out of the forty-six also bought domestic requirements, foodstuffs, flour, sugar, etc. Five did not state the annual amount of their purchases, but for those that did the amounts range from £100 to £75,000, the average being £17,000 to £18,000. The societies purchasing domestic goods appear to be among the smaller ones. The general societies may be taken to represent the average as well as the exceptionally high amounts of purchases. The dairy, fruit, and egg societies (except for one fruit society) are considerably below. This is, of course, because their main business is marketing, not the purchase of farmers' requirements. Of the societies which deal at all with the industrial movement, roughty six-sevenths of the general societies purchase from the C.W.S., but only one-third of the fruit societies and dairies. One of the egg societies is a C.W.S. customer for a small amount.

In the case of thirty-eight societies, it is possible to compare total sales of requirements to sales of requirements purchased from the C.W.S. The results are as follows:

```
8 societies sell 80–100 per cent. C.W.S. goods.
8    ,,      ,, 50–80     ,,    ,,    ,,    ,,
7    ,,      ,, 25–50     ,,    ,,    ,,    ,,
9    ,,      ,, 10–25     ,,    ,,    ,,    ,,
6    ,,      ,, under 10  ,,    ,,    ,,    ,,
```

There seem to be no special rules guiding the size or type of society which does proportionately the largest trade with the C.W.S. Of those buying more than 50 per cent. of their

requirements from the C.W.S. the majority are general
societies, but there are also four dairies and one fruit society,
which from a percentage point of view make exceptionally
heavy purchases. The largest gross purchase is 40 per cent.
of the society's total, but others standing at about the same
figure are not more than 17 per cent. of their respective
totals. The smallest gross purchase on record is also 40 per
cent. of total. Perhaps, on the whole, the medium-sized
societies are the best customers of the C.W.S. on a percentage basis, and among them may perhaps be reckoned
large societies whose main business is marketing. The
large societies, on the other hand, are actually larger gross
purchasers, but their mere size and higher organisation
gives them a wider choice and enables them to buy elsewhere
if the price suits them. They also buy goods, such as
machinery and imported feeding stuffs, which the C.W.S.
has less facility for supplying (See below.) Many of the
societies in this category are at the same time on unques-
tionably good terms with the C.W.S.

Before going on to discuss the purchases of the C.W.S.
from these societies, it would be well to say a word about
Wales. Out of a total of 92 societies (69 general, 17 dairy,
5 egg, and 1 fruit), 35 returns (two-fifths of the total) were
received. Of these 5 had ceased business, while 6 returned
blanks or negatived every question. Two of these negative
replies were from cheese societies, 4 from general traders.
The remaining 24 societies (2 dairies, 22 general), constituting
70 per cent. of the societies making returns, have more or
less important connections with the industrial movement.
All purchase agricultural supplies, and 13 also domestic

requirements from the C.W.S. in annual amounts varying in value from £150 to £30,000, but averaging about £9,000. The principal commodities purchased are, as in England, offals, meals, cakes, compounds, wheat, maize, seeds, manures and fertilisers, such as basic slag, superphosphates, etc., lubricating oil, coal, flour, hardware and groceries. The proportion of sales of C.W.S. to other goods is as follows:

```
5 societies sell 100 per cent. C.W.S. goods.
5     ,,         ,, 75–90    ,,    ,,    ,,    ,,
6     ,,         ,, 25–50    ,,    ,,    ,,    ,,
5     ,,         ,, under 25 ,,    ,,    ,,    ,,
```

The total sales of requirements for all Welsh societies in 1926 was £1,114,084, the total for the thirty-five societies making returns was £534,002 (50 per cent. of the trade thus coming from 40 per cent. of the societies), and the sale of C.W.S. goods by these thirty-five societies was £187,200, or 35 per cent. It will thus be seen that 70 per cent. of the societies trade with the C.W.S. to the extent of 35 per cent. of their trade.

Comparing these figures with those for England, it will be observed that, though there are nearly half as many societies in Wales as in England, their annual turnover in requirements is only one-fifth of that of England—that is to say, the turnover of an average Welsh society is only 40 per cent. of the turnover of an average English society. The proportion of societies dealing with the C.W.S. is practically the same, but where the average English society spends rather under £18,000 with the C.W.S., the Welsh society spends £9,000 or at least 10 per cent. more in proportion to its turnover. Thus the C.W.S. has a stronger hold on Wales than England, and the Welsh societies, though uniformly smaller than the English, are doing proportionately more trade in goods which are co-operative from their origin. Another peculiarity of the Welsh societies is the larger proportion of trade in domestic requirements. The reasons for these circumstances are, of course, the economic conditions of Wales; numerous small farms naturally result in numerous small co-operative societies, whose success and whose genuinely co-operative character are due to the work of the Welsh Agricultural Organisation Society. On the other hand, the agricultural districts in Wales are not extensively served by industrial co-operative societies, so that the farmers' societies naturally become distributors of groceries on a co-operative basis, and equally naturally the customers of the C.W.S.

Before leaving the subject of the C.W.S. supplies of agricultural requirements, it is worth considering how far it is possible to make a complete estimate of the trade involved. It has been possible to get very complete information for half the English societies and rather less than half of the Welsh, and it has been found that sales of C.W.S. goods form a certain percentage (26 per cent. in England and 35 per cent. in Wales) of the total sales of the societies. Applying this percentage to the total sales for both countries, we get £1,375,331[1] for England and (deducting something for sales of domestic goods) £370,000 for Wales—say, a total of £1,750,000. This is, of course, in retail prices. The C.W.S. estimate of their sales to farmers' societies is

[1] To this should be added about £7,000 from a society whose name is unascertainable, but which must be English or Welsh.

£1,500,000 in wholesale prices. It is possible that the societies which failed to reply are, on the whole, those with least to report, and also that the sales of domestic goods are larger than appear, both of which circumstances would tend to bring the two estimates even nearer together than they are. In any case they approximate sufficiently to make clear the general position of the C.W.S. as a farmer's provider.

It is now necessary to turn to the marketing side of agricultural co-operation and the functions of the industrial movement as a purchaser of farm produce. Of the 61 English farmers' co-operative societies under examination, 26 both buy from and sell to the industrial movement, 20 (which find their places amongst those just described) only buy, and 15 only sell. That is to say, 41 societies are engaged in marketing, and 46 in supplying their members' requirements.

The number of societies in England engaged in marketing produce on any scale is smaller than those supplying requirements (many supply societies now and then sell small parcels of members' produce, just as many marketing societies handle a limited amount of supplies). The total sales of produce, however, is £5,398,471, even without the sales of the large co-operative auction marts (principally for fruit), whose turnover cannot be calculated in the same way. This sum is nearly equal to the value of requirements handled by the societies, so that it is clear that the societies undertaking marketing are usually on a larger scale than those whose object is to supply requirements. The equality between these sums does not, however, represent anything in the nature of a balance of trade, as all the larger items making up these totals refer to different societies. It is only occasionally that a society is equally active in both directions, or that a supply society and a marketing society exist in the same district, duplicate their members, and so between them truly represent the sales and purchases of a body of farmers.

The societies replying to the questionnaire reported sales valued £1,482,445, which equals 27 per cent. of the total sales of produce. It would seem that many of the larger marketing societies did not reply to the questionnaire. Of this sum, produce to the value of £183,311, or 12 per cent., was sold to the C.W.S. as well as a certain quantity to retail societies.[1] It is significant that the proportion of produce sold to the C.W.S. is less than half that of the requirements purchased from it—that is to say, that 69 per cent. of the societies deal with the C.W.S.; they buy 26 per cent. of their requirements from it, and sell 12 per cent. of their produce to it. This indicates that though the C.W.S. is a valuable source of farmers' supplies, it is less valuable, or, alternatively, its value is less recognised, as a market for farmers' produce.

Of the 41 societies which sell to the industrial movement, 6 are fruit societies (six-sevenths of the fruit societies making

---

[1] It is extremely difficult to separate produce sold to the C.W.S. from produce sold to the retail societies, and all figures involving this distinction must, therefore, be taken as approximate.

A further difficulty is that two items (a) the sales of grain already mentioned in a footnote, and (b) the sales of requirements to retail societies discussed below, do not appear to find a place in the figures for total sales given by the Registrar of Friendly Societies. If they were given, they would probably still further reduce the estimate of 12 per cent., though how far is impossible to say.

returns), which, naturally, sell fruit, but in three cases also eggs; 9 dairy societies (three-quarters of those reporting) selling milk, cheese, and, in one case, butter; 1 egg society, and 24 general societies (three-fifths of those reporting), whose business may be divided as follows: 11 grain, 5 farmers' requisites, 2 potatoes, 1 wool, 1 fat stock and dairy produce. Of the 41 societies 9 may be said definitely to sell all or part of their produce to the retail industrial societies; 8 state equally definitely that their sales are to the C.W.S. For the purposes of general calculations, it has been assumed that the undescribed sales go in the main to the C.W.S. Those selling to the retail societies include 2 egg societies, 1 fruit society, and 1 fat stock and dairy; most of them also sell to the C.W.S. Amongst them are also 6 societies doing £24,800 worth of trade (out of a total of £47,000 worth of goods passing to the retail movement), who sell farmers' requirements to retail industrial societies. This is not, of course, marketing of produce in any sense; it is indistinguishable from the ordinary supply of requirements by an agricultural society to its members. It simply means that in these cases the local industrial society in its capacity as a farmer, grazier, or owner of horses, is a member of the local agricultural society, and purchases supplies from it. This trade is probably fairly large, though it is not easy to estimate its extent. It should certainly stand at twice the figures given. The question of the relations of farmers' societies with industrial societies will be treated at more length in the following chapter.

Of the 8 societies known to sell to the C.W.S., 2 sell grain, 2 fruit, 1 wool, 1 cheese, 1 potatoes, 1 fat stock and dairy produce. The total value of this trade (as far as figures are obtainable) is £69,416. Of this sum, however, £6,000 represents sales from two fruit auction marts. As the turn-over of these marts is not obtainable, this sum has been omitted from calculations aiming at comparisons and percentages.

Of the societies replying only thirty give the amount of their sales (omitting the above exceptional figure), which vary from £60 to £40,000, and average about £5,600. The grain and milk sales tend to be above the average, the requisites roughly upon it, and the fruit, eggs, wool, and potatoes, below. It may be noted that a good many of the societies selling grain have failed to state the annual amount, so that these sales may, in fact, modify the above statement. Probably also potatoes are a more important item of sale than appears by these figures. On the whole, the figures suggest that the largest gross sales to the C.W.S. are by societies which are in any case linked up to the C.W.S. by the purchase of requirements, and that the purely marketing societies have, with some exceptions, notably fruit societies, but a slight and casual connection with the industrial movement.

The proportion of C.W.S. to total sales in the case of individual societies varies greatly, but bears out this impression:

```
10 societies sell 90 to 100 per cent. to the industrial movement.
 4     ,,     ,,   50 to 70   ,,      ,,     ,,    ,,     ,,
14     ,,     ,,   under 25   ,,      ,,     ,,    ,,     ,,
```

The societies in the first category are almost all general societies, selling only comparatively small quantities of members' produce.   The last category contains most of the definitely marketing societies.   This does not reveal a hard-and-fast rule, but it indicates a tendency.

The sales to the industrial movement may also be looked at from the point of view of commodities which fall under the following heads:

Grain (wheat, oats, barley, rye, sometimes also grass seeds): supplied by 11 societies, total value about £80,000.

Fruit (fresh and sometimes canned, also vegetables, nuts, and flowers; eggs are sometimes sold by fruit societies, but are counted separately): supplied by 5 societies, total value £13,654.

Milk, with *Cheese* (a large item) and *Butter*: 10 societies, total value about £65,000 (3 societies supply milk only, 2 cheese only, 1 butter only, 3 milk and cheese, 1 milk, cheese, and butter).

Farmers' Requisites (chiefly fertilisers and feeding stuffs): 5 societies sell to retail industrial societies, total value £24,538.

Eggs: 4 societies, total £4,020.

Potatoes: 2 societies, total £2,600.

Wool: 1 society, total £800.

Fat Stock: 1 society, total about £20,000.

Turning to Wales it appears that the discrepancy between purchase from and sales to the industrial movement is even more striking than in England.   Taking all the societies for which information is obtainable, total sales of this type are only about one-seventh of total purchase; leaving out the many societies which do not market at all, the sales for those that actually do are about quarter of the purchases.

The total sales of produce by Welsh societies are small in themselves and in proportion to their business in requirements, showing that the marketing side of co-operation is comparatively little developed in Wales.   The figures are as follows:

		£
Milk and dairy produce		97,025
Eggs and poultry		25,261
Live stock		4,386
Dead meat		20
Fruit and market-garden produce ..		303
Sundries		135
	Total ..	£127,130

The societies replying to the questionnaire (about 40 per cent.) recorded £38,981 worth of sales, which amounts to 30 per cent. of the total, a somewhat higher proportion than that given by the English returns.   The point of interest, however, is that of these recorded sales £21,500, or 55 per cent. (against the English 12 per cent.), goes to the industrial movement.   These sales were effected by nine societies. Two are dairies, one doing a fairly large business, sells milk retail and grain to the C.W.S., and this accounts for almost its total sales (it is also a large purchaser of farmers' requirements from the C.W.S.); the other, a small society, sells about 13 per cent. of its cheese to the C.W.S. in some years, but not in all.   Seven general trading societies also sell potatoes, eggs, butter,[1] oats, wheat, barley and clover seeds to the industrial co-operative movement.   In one case the C.W.S. is specified, in another a retail society, but in most cases the purchaser is left indefinite.   The amounts

[1] The C.W.S. has a butter depot at Cardiff which purchases to some extent from Welsh farmers' societies.

vary from £100 to £10,000, and average about £2,400.   In all cases but two—the small dairy above mentioned and one large general society—all or practically all sales are to the industrial movements.

As all the Welsh societies under examination are considerable buyers of C.W.S. feeding stuffs, fertilisers, etc., it would appear probable that they have taken few conscious steps to develop marketing, but that being in close touch with them the C.W.S. itself has found it useful to pick up relatively small parcels of agricultural produce when they can be obtained through the society.   It is also possible that their sales are imperfectly recorded, and the proportion going to the C.W.S. is less overwhelming than it looks.

Assuming that 12 per cent. in England and 55 per cent. in Wales is the normal proportion of C.W.S. to general sales of produce by farmers' societies, it is possible to arrive at an estimated total of £674,809 in England (excluding the fruit auction marts), and £69,921 in Wales for these sales.   To this should be added, as an isolated amount, the £6,000 from the fruit marts, making a total of £750,730 purchased by the C.W.S. from organised agricultural producers.   Several rough estimates of this trade have been made by C.W.S. authorities which range from £300,000 to £400,000, to £1,000,000.   The variations may be due to the inclusion or omission of particular items, such as grain, but it must be understood that C.W.S. purchases are harder to estimate with precision than C.W.S. sales.   Certain known sales to the retail societies have been omitted from the above calculations; they amount to 25 per cent. of the corresponding C.W.S. sales, and their total may be estimated at about

£186,182. Added to the other figures this makes a grand total of £930,712, representing the sales of the agricultural to the industrial co-operative movement. If the fruit marts be once more omitted this leads to the general conclusion that *of the total trade of organised farmers in England and Wales, under 20 per cent. of their produce goes to the industrial co-operative movement, and rather over 30 per cent. of their supplies are derived from it.*

A few words may be said about the other relations between the two movements before passing on to give an account of particular societies. Of the societies in England replying to the questionnaire, 25 state that they are members of the C.W.S.; probably the number should be larger, as it is unlikely that societies doing insurance business and otherwise intimately connected with the C.W.S. are not members of that society; 14 both buy and sell; 11 buy only, and 2 sell only; 1 does neither, at least in the year under review· Purchase of supplies from the C.W.S. would thus appear to be a stronger inducement to membership than sales to it. This is natural, not only because the business involved is more extensive, but because membership secures an increased dividend on all purchases, but no corresponding advantage to the seller of produce. There are eight Welsh societies members of the C.W.S. The total number of societies members of the C.W.S. is known to about be ninety. One of the societies replying is a member of the Co-operative Union (there are actually about five agricultural members), and another of a local retail society. In several cases retail industrial societies are members of a farmers' society, sometimes taking a number of shares in it and receiving bonus on their purchases from it. (Farmers' societies also inter-trade to a certain extent with one another, particularly in grain, but that is somewhat outside the present enquiry.) Six Welsh and eighteen English societies insure with the Co-operative Insurance Society or are its agents. One or two societies make the C.W.S. their banker, and a certain number also use the services of its auditing department.

The facts point to certain general conclusions:

1. That the C.W.S. has a very considerable connection with farmers' co-operative societies, especially general societies, principally engaged in the supply of farm requirements.

2. That in many cases the terms on which these societies work with the C.W.S. differ neither in cordiality nor in extent of trade from terms of relationship between the C.W.S. and retail industrial societies.

3. That the connection between the specialised farmers' marketing societies and the C.W.S. is relatively slight, even amongst the comparatively few societies which exist.

4. That the connection between farmers' societies and retail industrial societies is also capable of great development.

5. That the farmers' societies in Wales,[1] smaller than in England, do a proportionately larger business with the C.W.S., particularly in connection with sales.

[1] The position in Scotland is entirely different. See chapter on Scotland.

FARMERS' SOCIETIES AND THE C.W.S.—*Continued.*

BEFORE leaving the subject of the C.W.S., it will be well to study the actual methods and recent history of a few representative farmers' societies in their relations with the industrial movement. In this, although the main emphasis is on their connection with the C.W.S., allusion must necessarily be made to their dealing with the retail societies, which will be treated in more detail in the next chapter. A certain repetition is unavoidable if each part of the narrative is to be complete.

THE SOUTHERN COUNTIES AGRICULTURAL TRADING SOCIETY, LIMITED.

This is a large society with its headquarters at Winchester. Its principal business is in farmers' requirements, which it sold to the value of £450,406 in 1926. In the same year it sold produce (chiefly wheat and eggs) to the value of £23,162. Meat, milk, and wool societies also exist in the district, and their members are to some extent also members of the Southern Counties. It is not known that they do any trade with the industrial movement. The society is increasing its business, but incurred heavy liabilities owing to the collapse of the A.W.S. It has rather under 1,000 members, but also sells to a large number of non-members, principally smallholders, who make satisfactory customers, and whom the society later hopes to enrol as members. Members are, on

104

the whole, loyal, and in the department of sales are generally willing to trust the disposal of their wheat entirely to the society. Besides supplying foodstuffs and fertilisers the society has an implement department. Only four farmers' co-operative societies have such a department, as the manufacturers will not sell except through those who will open a regular shop and stock spare parts.

The society was placed in a difficult financial position by the liquidation of the A.W.S., and its restoration to prosperity has been largely due to the help of the C.W.S. This has taken the form of trading credits and of a certain amount of advice in business management. At the same time the society has continued to obtain bank credits from the Midland Bank on the society's and various personal guarantees, and its policy is not under C.W.S. dictation. It is free to buy or not from the C.W.S. Agricultural Department, but it does, in fact, purchase feeding stuffs—bran, middlings, cake—seeds, seed-potatoes, coal, and fertilisers to the value of about £70,000 or roughly, one-sixth of its total purchases. Compounds are bought entirely from the C.W.S. to the amount of 3,000 tons. Certain forms of imported cake are not at present stocked by the C.W.S., but it is considering extension in that direction.

With regard to sales the society in ordinary seasons sells about one-third of its wheat (10,500 qrs. in 1926) to the C.W.S. In 1927 the quality was poor, and none was disposed of this way. The annual sales to the C.W.S. and the retail societies combined amounts to about £30,000. Sales to retail societies include oats, barley, and seeds in relatively small quantities, but also probably poultry food and similar agricultural requirements. A small quantity of poultry is sold to the C.W.S., and occasionally in glut seasons eggs are cold stored in private cold storage warehouses in Southampton and afterwards sold to the C.W.S. The main egg trade, however, is in graded and tested eggs supplied to shops in Southampton. The C.W.S. does not pay a sufficiently high price for fresh eggs of good grade to make it a profitable outlet. Many of the society's members sell milk direct to the C.W.S., but none passes through the society.

The society is satisfied with its connection with the C.W.S., and finds that both the agricultural accountant and organiser and some of the directors have a real understanding of agricultural co-operation. Some of the C.W.S. directors, however, whose experience has been mainly industrial, find it difficult to appreciate the need for allowing long credit to farmers. The society is an agent for the Co-operative Insurance Society, as well as for the Agricultural and General Insurance Society.

Dorset Farmers, Limited

This is a society of rather over 1,000 members with its headquarters at Dorchester. It is primarily a farmers' supply society, its turnover being accounted for almost entirely by sales of feeding stuffs, fertilisers, etc. It does not touch meat, milk, eggs, or wool. (Milk for the same area comes under the charge of the Sturminster Newton Society described below.)

Since the failure of the A.W.S. the society has become closely associated with the C.W.S. The C.W.S. is its banker and auditor, and allows considerable trading credits. It also appoints a representative to the Society's Board of Management. The society is not bound to purchase from the C.W.S., but in fact buys grass and root seeds, cake and offals to the value of £70,000 to £80,000. The goods are found to be of high quality, but usually slightly higher in price than those of other merchants. If the difference is marked, it is sometimes necessary for the society to purchase outside, while certain commodities are not readily obtainable from the C.W.S.

On the marketing side the society buys grain and seeds from its members, and sells a small quantity to the C.W.S., which gives it a certain preference, but is in no way bound to purchase. No considerable relations exist with retail societies, though the society would gladly extend its sales of poultry food through these channels.

The joint arrangement with the C.W.S. is considered satisfactory, and the C.W.S. personnel on the whole sympathetic. The heads of C.W.S. departments must, however, aim principally at making their own departments a commercial success, and are not unnaturally inclined to do so to the exclusion of any preferential treatment of co-operative societies, although this might be of ultimate benefit to the movement as a whole. The Dorset Farmers are anxious to see a still further development of inter-trading.

SOUTH DEVON FARMERS, LIMITED

This is a flourishing society on a somewhat smaller scale than the last two mentioned. It has a membership of 396 and total sales of about £30,000. It is a member of the C.W.S., and inter-trades very largely with it, but is not in

any way supervised or controlled, nor does it bank with
the C.W.S.   It purchases two-thirds of its supplies from the
C.W.S.   It also sells wheat on behalf of its members, and
in normal years almost all its sales of this commodity are
made to the C.W.S.   Barley, however, is disposed of to
local brewers, and meat, when it is handled at all, to local
butchers.   The society does not touch wool, but is thinking
of doing so.   The price of C.W.S. goods is considered high,
but it is neutralised by the payment of dividend on purchase.
The system of dividend payment is approved by the society.
The connection of the industrial movement with Labour
politics has been to some extent an obstacle to gaining the
farmers' confidence in the C.W.S.   The society has a retail
shop of its own which is commercially successful.   This is
naturally in competition with the local industrial society,
but no friction has arisen.   It is, however, doubtful if this
particular solution of the producer-consumer problem is
the best for general application.

The Cornwall and Wiltshire Farmers work in close connection with the C.W.S. on the same lines as the societies
just described.   The West Devon and North Cornwall
Farmers are in a similar position, as are also the North
Devon Farmers.   The feature of special interest in their
relations with the C.W.S. is their sales of fleeces, 1,000 to
2,000 annually from West Devon, to the C.W.S. Woollen
Mills at Buckfastleigh.   A certain number of fleeces are also
obtained from the Cornish Farmers.   These fleeces are not
bought and stored in bulk by the societies, nor is there
any attempt at grading.   The society simply buys from
members whenever it is sure of a customer.   The West

Devon Society also runs a slaughter-house from which all fells are sold at the C.W.S. fellmongery, which is also at Buckfastleigh. There is no general society covering the whole of Somerset.

STURMINSTER NEWTON FARMERS, LIMITED (DORSET)

This society is in a rather different position to the foregoing, as it is primarily a marketing society, selling milk to an annual value of about £134,800. The milk is collected by lorry from farmers within a ten-mile radius of Sturminster, cleaned and pasteurised, and sold principally to private merchants in London. The society formerly sold milk to the C.W.S., but this trade has come to an end owing to the establishment of C.W.S. milk depots in the western area. This has caused disappointment and a sense that the C.W.S. is a rival of the farmers' organisation, but at the same time the C.W.S. has been a useful financial ally, undertaking banking, auditing, and insurance for the society, also supplying goods (including petrol) to the value of £15,000 to £20,000 yearly, some of which are re-sold to the society's members. The society would willingly sell direct to the industrial movement if this could be done without giving umbrage to private customers, but the opportunity has not so far arisen.

Other instances of inter-trading in this district are the sale of eggs by the Melksham (Wilts) Society to the C.W.S. and the Sherton Co-operative Milling Society, which passes on any enquiries for requisites to the C.W.S. Two other societies in Wiltshire, one in Hants and another in Cornwall, are large purchasers from the C.W.S., and three dairies, two of them in Cornwall, sell milk to it. Going east into Surrey, Sussex, and Kent, the contact is much slighter. Some of the largest co-operative undertakings of this region are wool-marketing societies, which sell by auction and have little direct knowledge of their customers. As far as is known the C.W.S. is not among them.

EASTERN COUNTIES FARMERS' CO-OPERATIVE ASSOCIATION, LIMITED

This is a very large society with its headquarters in Ipswich, and branches all over the eastern counties. The society does a trade of £460,932 in farmers' requisites, and also sells produce to the value of £330,756; is affiliated to the C.W.S. and holds several shares in it. It also buys requisites considerably, but not exclusively, from the C.W.S., although its general attitude towards the industrial movement is a feeling of hostility, partly economic, partly political. The Ipswich Industrial Society is a member of the Eastern Counties Farmers, and buys feeding stuffs from it. The Farmers' Society also occasionally sells livestock, bacon, pigs, etc., to this or other co-operative societies. The trade, however, is not considerable, nor has it been especially cultivated. The eastern farmer is not enthusiastic about co-operation, although he may appreciate the business advantages of making use of a co-operative society, an attitude which does not encourage closer relations with the industrial movement.

Framlingham and Eastern Counties Co-operative Egg and Poultry Society, Limited

This is a large society (annual sales, £138,061, including certain sales of requirements; number of eggs sold, 20,390,626) covering much the same territory as the foregoing. It is a marketing society dealing in fresh and pickled eggs strictly graded, also in poultry, honey, game, and a little butter. It also buys feeding stuffs and poultry appliances for its members. It has a personal link with the industrial movement through its secretary, who is also Chairman (1928) of the Ipswich Industrial Society. It buys feeding stuffs, but not appliances, from the C.W.S. The C.W.S. prices are regarded as high, but the goods satisfactory. It also sells eggs to the Ipswich and other retail societies, and to the C.W.S., the latter sales being principally of pickled eggs. The C.W.S. insists on all pickled eggs sold to retail societies being invoiced through to itself. The Framlingham Society has retained the right to sell new-laid eggs direct, but in the case of pickled eggs the large purchases of the C.W.S. have made the concession worth while. The bulk of the society's trade, however, is still with private retailers, hotels, etc. It is possible to obtain a better price from this type of customer, partly because such customers require and will pay for a better quality egg, partly because they buy smaller quantities, and a selling society which will take the trouble to discover customers and supply them with the limited quantity required can secure a better price. The barrier to increased sales to the industrial movement is principally one of price and quality. The retail societies compete with the chain stores, and must supply a working-class clientèle at suitable prices.

STAMFORD AND DISTRICT EGG AND POULTRY SOCIETY, LIMITED

This is an egg marketing society of moderate size, but highly successful. It sold £1,787,000 of eggs in 1927 at a very low cost of handling, and realised good prices. The society operates over an area of about ten miles. It sells a comparatively small proportion of its eggs regularly to Long Eaton and Leicester Industrial Societies, and finds them very good customers, prompt and certain in payment. The C.W.S. does not offer a sufficiently high price for eggs to make trading profitable.

There remain three societies in the eastern district engaged in marketing fruit on a moderate scale, which all deal to some extent with the industrial movement. Two buy small quantities of requirements and one sells a small, the other a large, proportion of its fruit to the C.W.S.

PERSHORE CO-OPERATIVE FRUIT MARKET, LIMITED

This organisation sold by auction during 1927, £76,699 of produce, while classified and graded produce realised £3,552 by private sale. Considerable sales are effected to the C.W.S. depot at Cardiff, and the trade is a satisfactory one. The C.W.S. buys through a local agent who also acts for other buyers. The C.W.S. claims the right to act as agent for all the retail societies in South Wales. The Nottingham and Derby Societies buy direct from the market. The trade to the industrial movement is about £1,000 yearly, or 6 per cent. of the total.

LITTLETON AND BADSEY GROWERS, LIMITED

This fruit-marketing society sells on charge or on commission, but not by auction.   It has 340 members, and in 1927 sold produce worth £40,485.   About 16 per cent. of sales are to industrial societies, two-thirds of these on charge. The Co-operative Societies of *Worcester*, *Derby*, and *Ten Acres and Stirchley* are members of the society and receive bonus on purchase.   The growers' society is itself a member of the C.W.S., buys about £1,000 of fertilisers, etc., from it, and also has a satisfactory sale for vegetables and fruit to it. *Derby* Society sends regular orders and pays on a basis of retail prices actually received, not on the local market rate. " A perfect arrangement."   Annual trade about £2,000. The committee of *Ten Acres* trade with the society to about £1,000 annually as a matter of co-operative principle. *Leicester* takes produce on charge.

WORCESTERSHIRE FARMERS, LIMITED

This society has two departments, one carrying on the usual type of business in farmers' requirements with a turnover of £62,655 (1927), and the other a fruit and vegetable auction mart on the same lines as Pershore with a turnover of £25,923.   The requirements department buys very largely from the C.W.S. in feeding stuffs, seeds, and fertilisers, to the extent of about four-fifths of trade.   They are members of the C.W.S. and enjoy good relations with the industrial movement.   They do not market milk or meat.   The Auction Mart sells small quantities of fruit and vegetables, to the C.W.S. and the industrial societies.   Seeds are also sold through this department, all peas, beans, etc., being

8

bought from the C.W.S., but not seed potatoes, which they find can be bought more cheaply elsewhere.

SHROPSHIRE FARMERS' SOCIETY, LIMITED

This is a society with 1,150 members, supplying farmers with requirements and marketing their grain. It has a turnover of about £80,000. It is affiliated to the C.W.S. and holds shares in it. It buys offals and cake from the C.W.S. to the extent of about 30 per cent. of its turnover, and receives a bonus on these purchases. The society has never succeeded in selling grain to the C.W.S. under conditions which suit it. It does not handle perishables. Clover and grass seeds are both sold to, and bought from, the Eastern Counties Farmers' Association.

Two other fruit marts in the West Midland district sell each about £1,000 worth of produce to the industrial movement. A dairy society makes occasional sales of accommodation milk, and another society sells small quantities of eggs to the C.W.S. Four general societies buy from 14 to 60 per cent. of their requirements from the C.W.S., and two of these also sell a substantial proportion of their members' grain to the C.W.S.

In other parts of the Midlands eight general societies may be noted, all buying a substantial proportion of their requirements from the C.W.S. One of these also sells requirements to an industrial society, and three others sell a large percentage of a small turnover in members' produce to the industrial movement. Three dairy societies also make small sales of milk and cheese, and one cheese society parts with practically its whole stock to the local industrial society.

The Kidlington Bacon Factory (Oxon) does a profitable trade with the C.W.S.   One society has failed to sell grain to the C.W.S.; one dairy is definitely averse to any dealings with the industrial movement.

Preston and District Farmers' Trading Society

This is a large compact society with about 2,000 members and 6,000 customers, operating within a fourteen-mile radius of Preston.   The society's principal business is the sale of requirements, which reached a value of £426,243 in 1926.   The society has twenty-nine branches, and delivers feeding stuffs, etc., by lorry.   It also sells cheese, eggs, grain, and small quantities of straw on behalf of its members (value £73,562 in 1927).   The society is a member of the C.W.S. and trades very largely with it, having come to the conclusion, after experience, that intertrading is of mutual advantage.   The society buys large quantities of feeding stuffs from the C.W.S., but finds the price for millers' offals higher than that of private dealers, even when the dividend has been taken into account.   The society also sells a large quantity of cheese to the C.W.S. The C.W.S. makes it a condition of purchase that no cheese is sold to retail co-operative societies unless it is invoiced through the C.W.S.   The Preston Society acquiesces in this arrangement as the trade is valuable, but feels it to be inconvenient and uneconomic.   The society, though impressed with the co-operative purpose of the C.W.S. as a whole, is on its guard, as others are, against a tendency to departmentalism, and the setting of commercial interests above co-operative considerations in individual departments.

Lunesdale Farmers, Limited

This is another large society with headquarters at Lancaster. It sold in 1926 requirements to the value of £107,930, and produce to the value of £33,470. The society is a member of the C.W.S. and agent for the Co-operative Insurance Society. It buys 50 to 60 per cent. of its requirements from the C.W.S., and practically all its sales of produce are made to the industrial movement either wholesale or retail. They consist of fat stock—cattle, sheep, pigs —also dairy produce, milk, cheese, cream.

South-West Lancashire Farmers

This society—one of moderate size, doing rather more marketing than supply of requirements—has recently been able to establish satisfactory relations with the C.W.S. The society buys all its compounds from the C.W.S. African Oil Mills, and is an agent for the Co-operative Insurance Society. Members of the South-West Lancashire Society report that potatoes sold by them to private dealers have, in the past, been shipped direct from the farms to the C.W.S., but during the 1927 season a marked improvement took place, and the society received a fair amount of trade from the C.W.S. during the potato season of that year.

Two other dairy societies in Lancashire sell a small proportion of their produce to the industrial movement. One poultry supply society buys about 12 per cent. of its requirements from the C.W.S. Of two general societies one buys practically all, and the other 35 per cent., of its requirements from the C.W.S. The latter society also makes almost all its produce sales to the industrial movement.

Turning to Yorkshire it is necessary to make a sharp distinction between the industrial area of the West Riding and the purely agricultural districts.   In the industrial area the towns are set close together and completely fill the valleys. Farming is carried on by small farmers on the ridges of the hills, and is mostly dairy farming, egg, and pig production. There is no arable land.   The farmers have their market at their doors, or rather beneath their feet, and do most of their retailing themselves.   For this reason the industrial movement has made little progress in the milk business. Nor is there much development of co-operative marketing. On the other hand, a number of farmers' supply societies exist. It would appear superficially that their relations with the industrial movement and especially the C.W.S. should be close and cordial.   This, however, is not so.   The reason is that the local industrial societies have for some time dealt in farmers' supplies, principally feeding stuffs, which they can easily sell, as the farms are well within the industrial area, and some of them sell milk and offals.   They regard the farmers' societies, which are usually of more recent foundation, as interlopers, and also accuse them of under-selling.   In these circumstances the C.W.S. is, as far as can be ascertained, attempting to maintain impartiality, and it does, in fact, sell goods to the farmers' societies. However, as the latter do not place more than perhaps 10 per cent. of their orders with the C.W.S., and as the industrial societies, in any case much larger bodies, will place up to 75 per cent. of their orders with the C.W.S., the C.W.S. is naturally not disposed to offend the industrial societies by too extensive favours to their agricultural rivals.

Thus while several farmers' supply societies would willingly become members of the C.W.S., their applications have been refused. This is an unfortunate situation and one calling for discussion, tactful handling, and a wider view of co-operation.

In the agricultural districts the situation is entirely different. There is more marketing and a certain proportion of sales on satisfactory terms to the industrial societies. The societies, however, are geographically isolated; the C.W.S. is more or less unknown to them, and it has not made any special effort to push mutual relations. Consequently, though there is no hostility and no competition with the retail societies, the amount of trade from the C.W.S. to the farmers' societies is usually small. A few examples of both types of society may be quoted.

INDUSTRIAL DISTRICTS

CALDER VALE AGRICULTURISTS' TRADING SOCIETY.—This is a society with 323 members and a turnover of about £47,000, doing business entirely in farm requirements. It owns a mill on the Calder, and does its own grinding. A small proportion of the mill's requirements are bought from the society's own members. The society makes slight purchases from the C.W.S., but closer relations are impeded by the fact that it is in competition with other co-operative milling undertakings in the neighbourhood. It has applied for membership of the C.W.S., but the application has been refused owing to the opposition of local industrial societies. The society finds that it can buy C.W.S. offals more profitably through brokers than direct. The society has a few of the smaller retail societies among its members, and sells feeding stuffs, etc., to them. The retail societies also buy milk, dairy produce, etc., from individual members of the society. They are good customers, and pay promptly and with certainty.

WAKEFIELD FARMERS' SOCIETY.—This society has 602 members and a turnover of about £30,000. It has a grinding mill. It has occasionally bought small quantities of offals from the C.W.S., and has also sold grain to the local industrial society, but, on the whole, it is detached from and indifferent to the industrial movement.

SOWERBY BRIDGE DAIRY FARMERS' ASSOCIATION.—This is a society of ninety members, with a turnover of £16,856, principally in cattle-feeding stuffs. It does no marketing. The society buys 25 per cent. of its requirements from the C.W.S. The price is satisfactory, but the quality does not altogether suit the members. The society would like to be a member of the C.W.S., but is excluded owing to the opposition of the local industrial society which has itself a flour-mill and sells feeding stuffs to farmers. The Sowerby Bridge Society gets a half dividend on its purchases from the C.W.S. The local industrial society formerly sold milk from its own farm and dairy at a lower price than that charged by individual farmer-retailers. It made a loss and abandoned the attempt.

HALIFAX FARMERS' TRADING ASSOCIATION.—This is a society with a turnover of about £42,577, carrying on the supply of feeding stuffs and other requirements, and also milling. The society makes small purchases from the C.W.S., but is deterred from closer association by the attitude of local industrial societies, and by a diffidence arising out of its recent losses in the A.W.S. collapse.   There is keen competition in this district between industrial and agricultural societies for the farmers' trade.

Another farmers' society in the Halifax district does a variable amount of trade with the C.W.S.

AGRICULTURAL DISTRICTS

These may be more summarily dealt with.   Of four small societies in the dales, one is a marketing society, manufacturing and selling cheese, a fair proportion of which goes to retail industrial societies.   Another dairy society is a member of the Co-operative Union, but does not appear to have any trading relations with the industrial movement. One general trading society does a very large proportion of its trade with the C.W.S., another a mere fraction, coupled with an even smaller sale of produce.

THE TEESIDE FARMERS, LTD., have their headquarters in Darlington, but actually serve a portion of the North Riding.   The society is a large one, with one 800 membership and a turnover of £219,365.   The society has no extensive relations with the industrial movement, merely buying small quantities of offals from the C.W.S. and selling small quantities of grain to the C.W.S. and retail societies.   It is, however, sympathetic to the idea of closer relations with the industrial movement.

Other farmers' societies in the north include a fairly large society in Northumberland, which makes about one-third of its purchases from the C.W.S., and sells considerable quantities of agricultural requirements to local industrial societies, a general society in Cumberland, purchasing considerably from the C.W.S., but not a member of it, and a dairy society which, in proportion to a small turnover, buys considerable quantities of bran and meal from a retail industrial society.

There is comparatively little to be added to what has already been said of societies in Wales.   A certain proportion of produce is frequently sold to the industrial movement, and a large number of societies buy requirements from the C.W.S. The societies buying wholly from the C.W.S. are generally small ones, and a lack of alternative sources of supply has something to do with their fidelity.   There may be a tendency amongst some of these societies to lay their burdens too much on the shoulders of the C.W.S., to the weakening of their own self-reliance.   A few societies, including some larger ones, have been saved from liquidation by the action of the C.W.S., and receive its financial support. The C.W.S. has an agent in South Wales whose work is appreciated.   The political policy of the Co-operative Union is causing some uneasiness amongst farmers, and may even have affected inter-trading.   The distinction between the agricultural and industrial movements in Wales is very fluid, and there is a tendency for the two to merge together. Many of the small agricultural societies, especially in isolated districts, do nearly 40 per cent. of their business in domestic goods.   Occasionally these societies have been absorbed by an industrial society, in one case the industrial has been absorbed by the agricultural society.

THE RETAIL SOCIETIES AND THE FARMER

THE Retail Co-operative Societies are the largest consumer unit in the country, and they are constantly growing. They are self-governing and self-conscious, and they are animated by definite social ideals. For these reasons they have an actual and still more a potential influence on the farmers' market which is unique.

In 1926 there were in Great Britain and Ireland 1,280 retail distributive societies with a membership of 5,186,728 persons. Of these 4,461,921 were in England and Wales, 677,258 in Scotland, and 47,549 in Ireland, where industrial co-operation on a large scale is practically confined to the Belfast neighbourhood. When the last census was taken in 1921 the membership of retail co-operative societies was 10 per cent. of the population in England, 13 per cent. in Scotland, 6 per cent. in Wales, and, for the reason stated, less than 1 per cent. in Ireland. Since that year the total membership has increased by half a million. The members of retail co-operative societies are usually the heads of families, so that the percentage of the population actually fed through the movement is probably four times as great— say, 21,000,000.

In the year 1926 the total trade of the retail co-operative societies was £184,879,702. The societies in England and Wales accounted for £148,812,556 of this sum, the Scottish societies for £34,380,485, and the Irish for £1,686,661. To understand what this buying power means to the farmer, it is necessary to analyse the figures further. The trade of the Co-operative Wholesale Society is 50 per cent. of that of the retail societies in England, and the trade of the Scottish Wholesale Co-operative Society about 40 per cent. of that of the Scottish retail societies. The sales of wholesale and retail societies, however, are reckoned respectively in wholesale and retail prices. This means that the actual percentage of retail societies' purchases from the wholesales is considerably higher—probably at least 55 per cent. of their total trade. In Scotland the percentage is probably as high as in England, as the gap between retail and wholesale prices tends to be higher in the co-operative movement of that country. A further indeterminate factor is the C.W.S. sales to agricultural societies at home or abroad. It may be taken that approximately £82,000,000 worth of produce sold in retail co-operative stores in England, and £19,000,000 in Scotland, is purchased from the Co-operative Wholesale Societies. It consists mainly of groceries, of which the important items from the agriculturist's point of view are flour, bacon, butter, cheese, eggs, dried and hard fruits, and jam. Tea, tobacco, and margarine do not at present affect co-operative agriculture. In addition the C.W.S. supplies milk to a fairly large extent, also a variety of non-foodstuffs in smaller amounts, the most important of which to the agriculturist are woollen and leather goods.

There remains produce to the value of roughly £66,000,000 in England and £15,000,000 in Scotland, which is not derived from the wholesale societies. Of this, £25,647,271 in England

and £7,396,733 in Scotland represents products and services of the retail societies themselves.

The comparatively small sums of £460,454 in England and £180,386 in Scotland represent produce from retail societies' own farms. There are 123 societies in England and 20 in Scotland which farm respectively 39,348 and 9,488 acres—the English societies only produce in this way goods to the value of less than 0·4 per cent. of their total sales. In Scotland the figure is about 0·5 per cent. The majority of these farms do not pay, and there has been a slight decline in farming by the industrial co-operative societies in recent years. It may be observed that 11 of these farms are for grazing purposes only, and are properly a charge on the butchery department; 61 show a surplus before the deduction of interest and depreciation, only 26 do so after this deduction has been made.

The comparative failure of this kind of co-operative farming is attributed to various causes. The reasons most usually accepted are: (1) that the farms are managed by bailiffs under a managing committee of townsmen; (2) that the manager's salary is a charge on a farm, which in the case of an independent farmer would go down as profit; (3) that co-operative societies' farms are run on a lavish scale as regards wages, repairs, etc.; (4) that the farm accounting, by making heavy allowances for depreciation and in other ways, tends to present the results in their worst light; (5) that societies bought their farms in most cases directly after the war, when land was at an inflated value, and like other farmers in similar cases have suffered from the ensuing slump. It has also been suggested that the want of the personal touch, sense of ownership, etc., involved in company farming, is a predisposing cause of failure.

Farming by co-operative societies has not been wound up, nor is it likely to be altogether abandoned. It may even increase; but at present at least the tendency in the industrial movement is to look for the development of co-operative agriculture along other lines, and to regard the retail societies' own farms as experiments, a check upon agricultural prices and a means of understanding the farmers' problems.

There remains in England £25,186,817 and in Scotland £7,216,347 worth of goods and services produced by the retail societies unaccounted for. This covers processing of various kinds, bakery, jam-making, sometimes flour-milling, dress-making, etc. It frequently concerns some sort of agricultural product used as a raw material, but it introduces an element of great uncertainty into statistical calculations; for instance, in the case of baking, the flour is usually a C.W.S. product, and its value is thus in danger of being reckoned twice.

A number of co-operative societies exist in Great Britain which are engaged in industrial production, but which are controlled by the workers in the industry rather than the consumers of the product, and thus resemble the farmers' societies in their economic structure and bias in favour of the producers. Unlike the farmers' societies, they work in the closest touch with the industrial consumers' movement, practically all their produce being sold either to the C.W.S. or the retail societies. The trade of these societies amounts to £3,806,747 in England and £1,933,494 in Scotland.

It is probable that the bulk of these sums represents sales to retail societies, and should therefore be counted amongst the figures for goods of co-operative origin handled by these societies. Here again, however, caution must be exercised in judging the figures, as the C.W.S. or S.C.W.S. will not infrequently have supplied the raw material to the producers' society. In Scotland the types of production of interest to agriculturists are baking and confectionery (£1,572,993), for which the flour is almost certainly from the S.C.W.S., and thus represents no separate demand, and textiles (£293,415), a smaller item, but one for which the S.C.W.S. is much less likely to supply the raw material. In England there are societies engaged in textile manufacture (£1,388,326), boot-making and leather (£715,561), baking and confectionery (£323,638), and corn milling (£214,670), all of which use raw materials derived from agriculture; of these only baking and confectionery societies are likely to be supplied with raw materials in bulk by the C.W.S.

When all the foregoing deductions have been made there remains the sum of about £37,000,000 in England and £6,000,000 in Scotland, which represents goods bought by the retail co-operative societies direct from farmers, manufacturers and others unconnected with the industrial co-operative movement. These sums, it must be remembered, are calculated in retail, not in wholesale prices, and they represent considerably less to the producers of the goods in question. It is not easy to say precisely what is included amongst these goods. Societies are not invariably " loyal to the C.W.S."; some buy clothing or proprietary goods from private merchants, but it is safe to say that a large proportion consists of perishables of agricultural origin. The retail society buys to a very large extent its milk, meat, green vegetables and fruit, sometimes also smaller quantities of cheese, butter, or grain, direct from local farmers, from farmers' organisations, or on the market. It is with purchases of this type that the present chapter is principally concerned.

As long ago as 1909, when the industrial co-operative movement was at less than half its present strength, an attempt was made to enquire into its relations with agriculture. In a pamphlet, "Agricultural Co-operation," published by the Co-operative Union in that year, a good deal of information was collected. Four big societies— Leeds, Plymouth, Bradford City, and Gateshead were all described as large buyers of all kinds of agricultural produce including fruit and vegetables. Pendleton, Newcastle, and Bolton also bought agricultural produce, chiefly cereals and roots; Crewe made large purchases direct from local farmers; Norwich bought £3,000 worth of dairy produce, fruit, and vegetables locally; Derby did a very large egg and milk trade; Lincoln bought £8,272 worth of butter and eggs from its own members. One society, that of Wickham Market, which appears to have since been dissolved or amalgamated, had a regular scheme for collecting eggs from members by the same carts that delivered groceries and afterwards marketing those not required for the Society's own members.

In 1916 the Co-operative Survey report casts a further light on the position. In that year 123 societies in England and Scotland sold milk, 38 greengrocery, 16 (11 in Scotland) fruit, and 8 grain and corn. A few societies also had a florist's department; some dealt in agricultural implements, artificial manures, seeds, feeding stuffs, lime, eggs and poultry (the latter apparently for breeding purposes). On the productive side 73 societies had farms, 94 undertook slaughtering and butchering, 35 sausage making, 10 bacon curing, 26 corn milling, and 9 dairying. A few societies manufactured bone, meat, and blood manure, made butter or carried on market gardening. Almost all these activities have greatly increased since 1916. Since then the milk trade in particular has greatly developed, and in 1927 it was recorded that 300 societies had opened milk departments and sold from £5,000,000 to £6,000,000 worth of milk in the course of the year.

It is not possible to-day to get a complete statistical statement of the retail co-operative societies' relations with agriculture, but by studying the practice of a number of representative societies, both agricultural and industrial, a fair idea of prevailing conditions may be obtained.

As has been noted in a previous chapter, the number of agricultural societies which state definitely that they deal with a retail society is small, and in practically every case their dealings take the form of sales to the latter; only one records a purchase of feeding stuffs *from* an industrial co-operative society. The purchases of retail societies from agricultural societies fall into two classes: (1) In a number of cases the retail industrial society is a member of the agricultural society, and purchases from it poultry foods and other feeding stuffs, fertilisers, etc., either for its own farms or for re-sale to members in the smallholder and " back-yarder " categories. (2) A more interesting development is the purchase of dairy produce, grain, meat, eggs, fruit and vegetables by the retail society from an agricultural society which is engaged in marketing such produce on behalf of its members.   At a rough estimate the trade in requirements which passes through the hands of farmers' societies to retail societies may amount to £80,000.   The value of agricultural produce sold to the retail societies is almost impossible to estimate, involved as it is with the same societies' sales to the C.W.S.   Individual instances, however, may be given as characteristic.

Several fruit and vegetable marketing societies in the Midlands sell fairly large quantities of these commodities, and also of eggs, to retail societies in the same district.   The Anglesey Egg Society did a considerable trade with distributive societies who were large purchasers of first quality eggs.   One Welsh society sold milk retail, and one potatoes. A West of England farmers' slaughter-house carries on a considerable trade with the local industrial society.   The Midland Marts, Ltd., a farmers' live-stock auction, carried on on co-operative lines, but not registered under the Industrial and Provident Societies Acts, does about one-fifth of its business with retail societies, who are amongst its largest and most constant buyers, and have given the Mart valuable support from its inception.   A large farmers' society in the Eastern Counties occasionally sells fat stock, pigs, and bacon for its members to local retail societies, but the trade is occasional and no special efforts are made to develop it.   An egg society (Framlingham and Eastern Counties) in the same neighbourhood sells a fairly large quantity of eggs to the local society and some to industrial

9

societies in other areas.   Pickled eggs are invoiced through
the C.W.S., but fresh eggs are sold direct.   A few societies
sell milk and milk products, especially cheese.   One farmers'
society in the north writes of the industrial co-operative
societies: " We seek to cater for them by reason of the fact that
we know they are able to pay as good a price as anybody else
and take large quantities."   The same society has persuaded
certain industrial societies to give their members priority when
buying fat stock.   " Cattle are bought in the usual way and
sent direct to the Industrial Co-ops. for immediate slaughter.
Direct trade is established and is proving very satisfactory to
all concerned."   It must also be borne in mind that certain
sales are effected by overseas farmers' co-operative organisations direct to some of the larger industrial societies.

Besides the agricultural societies there are a very large
number of farmers who sell direct to the industrial movement, and some of these have organised themselves or been
organised by the retail societies into loose associations.

To understand not only the actual position with regard to
the retail societies' relations with agriculture, but also its
possibilities of development in the co-operative sense, an
analysis of the buying methods of a number of societies may
not be without value.

Derby Co-operative Provident Society

An example of perhaps the most complete and conscious
attempt to co-operate with organised farmers, this society
(1927 membership, 46,572; sales, £2,067,907; share capital,
£983,314), under the guidance of a former manager, deliber-
ately set out to be as much a rural as an urban movement.

It aimed at an extensive rural membership to whom it would act as provider, and at purchasing its supplies either from its own country members or from organised bodies of farmers. It buys to a very large extent from the C.W.S., but of what remains about 80 per cent. comes from its own members. Some details will show the progress that has been made.

CHEESE.—In 1900, 85 per cent. of the cheese sold by the society was imported; by 1913 this proportion had been reduced to less than 1 per cent. Special efforts were made to encourage local production, and the society to-day purchases practically the whole supply of the Manifold Valley Dairy Association.

EGGS were formerly bought from dealers on the Ashbourne and Uttoxeter markets. Since 1901 the society has had its own egg depot, and purchases direct from the producers. About 50 per cent. of the eggs required are collected by the grocery carts on their rounds. A great increase has taken place in the number of eggs purchased, and also in the proportion of English eggs to imported.

VEGETABLES are still bought on the market, but an arrangement also exists with the smallholders' societies.

GREEN FRUIT was formerly bought from wholesale fruiterers and commission agents. These wholesalers had often purchased orginally from co-operative producers, and before the Derby Society entered the fruit business, members of that society would buy fruit from co-operative producers after it had passed through the hands of private wholesalers and retailers. Supplies are now derived from: (1) members with farms or gardens; (2) smallholders' societies in Derbyshire, Worcestershire, and Gloucestershire; (3) C.W.S.;

(4) Pershore Fruit Market and Littleton and Badsey Growers. Dove Valley damsons are collected from farmer members by the society, which sends out empties on milk lorries to the dairy depot. The farmers fill them and send them into Derby with the next milk delivery.

MEAT is bought from members to a limited extent, but the Society would gladly purchase from organised farmers if the opportunity arose.

MILK.—The society started dairying on farms of its own which, though still retained, have long been inadequate. It now handles 31,000 to 32,000 gallons per week, entirely supplied by farmers, members of the Derby Society. The society calls an annual Conference of supplying farmers at which the price is fixed for the ensuing year. The price varies from 10d. in the summer to 1s. 3¾d. per gallon in the winter. The milk is supplied from a six-mile radius, and 75 per cent. is collected by the society's lorries, ⅜d. per gallon being charged for collection. The milk is sold loose (not bottled) at 4½d. in summer and 6d. per quart in winter. The society's business accounts for 80 per cent. of the total Derby milk supply.

AGRICULTURAL REQUIREMENTS.—The society sells seed, fertilisers, etc., to its farmer members to the value of £20,000 yearly.

The rural policy of the Derby Society is best given in a quotation from a book, " Seventy-five Years' Co-operation in Derby," recently published by the society.

" The ideal for which the Derby Society now strives is the obtaining of land for smallholdings and the turning of the attention of educational bodies to the encouragement of the right class of men (that is, the agricultural labourers) in our villages to apply for such land and organise their labours in co-operative groups.

" When this is done the distributive societies' motors can with ease serve districts 25 or 30 miles from the central premises. They could take out a load of groceries and provisions, feeding stuffs for cattle, seeds, patent manures, etc., and on the return journey bring a load of pigs, sheep, hay, straw, fruit, vegetables, eggs, milk, or cheese. All this could be done were producers grouped together in co-operative colonies. . . . Motor traffic is now common to all parts of the country, but few business firms are able to make it as remunerative as co-operative societies. The requirements of the Derby Society, as an instance, are so varied that motors can be kept constantly employed, which is a matter of vital importance.

" There then is the ideal the Derby Society has set before it. It is an ideal which concerns intimately every individual member of the Society; it concerns also co-operative principles that have, to some extent, been neglected in the past. Towards the realisation of that goal the society in 1924 had steadily set its path, because it leads down an avenue of success, both in business and in the making of each individual life."

ROYAL ARSENAL (WOOLWICH) CO-OPERATIVE SOCIETY

The Royal Arsenal Co-operative Society is one of the largest in England, and caters for the greater part of London south of the Thames. It had in 1927 a membership of 201,204, and its share capital stood at £1,908,502. For the year 1927 its sales totalled £6,243,950, and in the same period it paid to members a patronage dividend of £442,323. It had departments dealing in every form of agricultural

produce whose methods can best be described if each depart
ment is taken separately.

All figures refer to 1927.

MILK—*Sales of Dairy Department*, £383,854.—Milk is
bought entirely through the C.W.S., which in turn purchases
it from individual farms in Somerset, Wilts, and other
counties, collects it at local depots, and dispatches it,
largely in glass-lined tanks, by road to Woolwich, where it
it is cleaned and pasteurised. The amount stands at 80,000
gallons a week, and represents a large proportion of the
C.W.S. milk business. The C.W.S. pays carriage up to the
Woolwich Society's premises. It buys the milk at current
rates, and charges a certain commission to cover cost of its
services. If there is any surplus on the year's trading, it is
returned to the retail society as bonus (or dividend) on
purchase in the usual way. The Royal Arsenal Society in its
turn sells at the current price, and distributes surplus in the
form of dividend on purchase to its members. Now the
society is increasing the practice of distributing the milk
in bottles, sold at the same price. The farmer receives no
particular benefit unless the C.W.S. price is an improvement
on that offered him by other wholesalers.

MEAT—*Sales* £606,911.—The home meat trade has not increased greatly since the War, but the overseas trade is much
larger. The bulk of the home meat comes from Essex,
Suffolk, and Norfolk. The society's buyer has a pass on the
Great Eastern Railway, and goes round buying direct from
individual farmers. Other meat is bought in the market
or through the C.W.S., which itself buys very much in the
same way.

FLOUR—*Purchases of Bakery Department, £177,900.*— Fifty-nine per cent. of the total purchases of flour are from the C.W.S.

FRUIT AND VEGETABLES—*Sales of Greengrocery Department, £96,211.*—The society owns a farm which is used for the production of small quantities of fruit, vegetables, and eggs. It does not pay, however. A small amount is also bought from the C.W.S., including all the Jamaica bananas stocked by the society. The C.W.S. have their own ripening rooms for bananas; if the Royal Arsenal Society had sufficient space they could equally well carry out this process themselves, and would save money on it. About 25 per cent. of hard fruits are bought direct from Kentish farmers. The society's buyer goes round the orchards choosing the fruit on the trees. The society has a buyer with an office in the Borough Market, and the bulk of their greengroceries, with the above exceptions, are purchased there. Soft fruits are said to be in better condition when bought on the market than those which can be purchased direct from individual farmers. Bananas from the Canaries are bought on the market, also citrus fruits from South Africa, Canada, and the U.S.A. These are probably largely of co-operative origin, but are not bought direct from co-operators. Buying in the market is from two or three commission agents who are well known to the buyer, and the society finds this method satisfactory for its own purposes. The society has a *Preserve Factory* (production, £99,226) which buys a considerable quantity of fruit direct from Kentish farmers. The factory makes jam and also bottles fruit. Any extra jam required is purchased almost entirely from the C.W.S.

BACON.—This is purchased green from the C.W.S. and smoked by the society, though some is purchased ready smoked.   Much of this is doubtless from co-operative sources in Denmark and Ireland.   The society has a small account with the Co-operative Bacon Factory at Bury St. Edmunds.

EGGS.—These are purchased on the London market, a few, however, are from the Overseas Farmers' Co-operative Federations.

CHEESE.—English cheese is bought from the C.W.S., which buys from farmers in the Somerset district.   Imported cheese is almost entirely of co-operative origin, and is roughly in the proportion of two-thirds from New Zealand and one-third from Canada, with a small amount from Australia. Dutch cheese (Edam) is also largely of co-operative origin.

It will be observed that the Royal Arsenal Society makes no special efforts to get into touch with farmers or farmers organisations.   The society's membership is entirely urban, and it is even geographically cut off from the countryside. It does make a definite effort to deal with the C.W.S. wherever possible.   It has various contacts with farmers, strictly in the way of business, and in the same way purchases very considerably, though sometimes indirectly, from overseas farmers' co-operative organisations.

LONDON CO-OPERATIVE SOCIETY

The London Co-operative Society serves London north of the Thames.   In 1927 it had a membership of 222,238, its capital stood at £2,250,612, and its sales for the half year ending September, 1927, were £2,929,093.   It paid £144,000 in dividends on purchase to members for the same period.

The society is especially anxious to be on good terms with the farmer, to enter into definite relations with him, and to assure him the fairest treatment. It has succeeded in making some arrangements with dairy farmers which would appear to be mutually satisfactory, but its leaders insist that the next move lies with the farmer, that co-operative organisations must be formed on his side and produce sold of a quality (and quantity) and in a form acceptable to the consumer.

MILK—*Sales half year*, 1927, 2,547,394 gallons.—The society does not buy through the C.W.S., but has always dealt direct with farmers. Originally it bought at the N.F.U. contract price, but about five years ago the society started to bring the farmers supplying it into a loose organisation. A few farmers were interested at first, but the movement has grown, and now the price is fixed annually between the London Society and an informal Committee of farmers. The custom is for the society to take all the milk the farmer has to offer at liquid price, and pay an additional ½d. per gallon over the current rate. The farmers' contract to supply a certain quantity of milk at each period of the year, but are allowed to vary it by 20 per cent. under, or 10 per cent. over, the stated amount. Beyond these limits the society reserves the right to pay at a different rate, but has never exercised it. At one time considerable losses to farmers occurred through sour milk, and the society has now started a creamery at Buckingham, where the milk is collected and treated, and whence it is dispatched in glass-lined tanks to London. The society inspects supplying farms periodically, and is well satisfied as to cleanliness, etc. A similar system is carried out in Essex, but there there is no common action amongst the farmers, and their relations with the society are less friendly and more purely commercial.

EGGS AND BUTTER.—An attempt is to be made this year (1928) to collect eggs and butter in Buckinghamshire on the same lines as milk. At present both commodities are bought partly through the C.W.S. (both English and blended butter), and partly from importers. A small quantity of eggs are bought from the Framlingham Co-operative Egg and Poultry Society.

FLOUR, JAM, AND DRIED FRUIT are purchased from the C.W.S., so is cheese (although small quantities come direct from farmers in Somerset).

BACON.—This is mainly derived from Denmark and Ireland. Danish bacon is cheaper than English, and is preferred by the co-operative public. The society is also arranging to buy bacon from the Leicester (Industrial) Society, which is starting a large bacon factory.

MEAT—*Sales of Butchery Department, £228,791.*—Of this, 70 per cent. is English, and is bought direct from farms by the society's buyer.

The society would gladly open contra accounts with the farmers supplying milk and other commodities, and would supply them with feeding stuffs, fertilisers, etc. However, the Buckingham area (the most promising from this point of view) is in the Bletchley (Industrial) Society's district; according to co-operative regulations the London Society would not be justified in selling in the Bletchley Society's district, and attempts to get the farmers to trade with the Bletchley Society have not as yet been particularly successful.

MANCHESTER AND SALFORD CO-OPERATIVE SOCIETY

The Manchester and Salford Society (membership in 1928, 37,157; sales, £1,574,231) has not made any special efforts to get into touch with farmers, except in the milk business. The society handles 28,000 gallons of milk weekly, all of which is bought direct from about 130 individual farmers widely scattered over a large area.   Prices are fixed annually by the north-western section of the Co-operative Union in consultation with the N.F.U.   The milk is collected by private vans (the farms supplying are too scattered to make co-operative transport feasible), which also collect eggs and sometimes meat for co-operative and also private firms and bring it into Manchester.   Large quantities of eggs are bought in this way, and the society only buys to a very limited extent on the market.   Meat was formerly bought on the market, but an attempt is now being made to collect it in the same way as milk and eggs.

NORWICH CO-OPERATIVE SOCIETY

This society is situated in the centre of an agricultural district, and has members engaged in farming and market gardening.   Before the War a very large quantity of Norfolk butter was sold by the society, but this trade has dwindled and been replaced from Danish sources through the C.W.S. Bacon and flour are also bought from the C.W.S., and milk comes from the C.W.S. depot at Claydon, though it is cleaned and pasteurised by the society.   Meat is largely bought at markets, though to a certain extent it comes direct from the farm.   Butter, eggs, fruit and vegetables are still bought in fairly large quantities from the society's own members.

Produce is collected by the grocery carts while making their rounds. The society sells chicken food to its members, but no other form of agricultural requirement.

CAMBRIDGE CO-OPERATIVE SOCIETY

The society purchases 75 per cent. of its milk supplies direct from dairy farmers, and 75 per cent. of its meat straight from the farm. From the C.W.S. it buys 60 per cent. of its flour, 100 per cent. butter, and 95 per cent. bacon. All tomatoes, potatoes (except early Jerseys), and fresh eggs are bought from smallholders who are members of the society.

BIRMINGHAM CO-OPERATIVE SOCIETY

Share capital, £1,059,379; sales, £3,672,379; membership, 125,639 (1927). This is a very large society working in an industrial area and hemmed in by other industrial societies and areas, so that it has practically no geographical contact with the country. The society has a small farm which makes a slight loss. The proportion of purchases of co-operative origin in the different departments are of some interest: grocery, 70·3 per cent.; restaurant, 42·7 per cent.; bakery, 53·5 per cent.; confectionery, 7·4 per cent.; boots, 55·6 per cent.; drapery, 51·3 per cent.; tailoring, 78·5 per cent.; furnishing, 52·8 per cent.; butchery, 13·5 per cent.; dairy, 0·1 per cent.; fish, fruit, and greengrocery, 1·0 per cent.; farm requirements, 14·8 per cent.; coal, 44·1 per cent. It will be observed that the proportion is lowest in the purely agricultural departments.

MILK.—The society has a large dairying business (45,000 gallons weekly), and practically all their milk is bought direct from individual farmers, very few of whom are members. The farmers have a Dairymen's Association with which the society negotiates the contract for each year. This contract has slightly raised the price for the farmers above what they were formerly getting. Transport is arranged by the farmers. Other retail societies in the district buy in the same way.

MEAT.—The society is hampered in developing its own slaughtering by the fact that the Corporation abattoirs control the situation, and independent licences are difficult to obtain. The society hires premises at the Corporation abattoirs, and slaughters beasts bought at the live-stock market from dealers or from farmers; it also buys meat on the dead-meat market. About 10 per cent. of supplies are derived from the Midland Marts. English meat sold by the society represents about 50 per cent.

CHEESE.—English, mainly from the C.W.S. at Bristol.

EGGS.—From wholesalers and importers.

BUTTER.—New Zealand, Irish, Danish; mainly from the C.W.S.

GREEN FRUIT AND VEGETABLES.—The department was established nine years ago. There was an attempt to buy direct from the growers, but the policy was a commercial failure and was discontinued. All purchases are now made in the Birmingham market.

AGRICULTURAL DEPARTMENT.—A few years ago a Seeds and Feeding Stuffs Department was set up with a view to selling to members and also farmers, especially milk suppliers. Little progress, however, was made, and the farmers' trade was considered " hazardous "—i.e., very long credit was required.

Ipswich Industrial Co-operative Society

This society had in 1927 a membership of 24,112, and a year's sales amounting to £843,399. Its agricultural policy and connections have some points of interest. The society has analysed the source of its supplies as follows: 60·5 per cent. from the C.W.S., 5·8 per cent. from other co-operative sources, 33·7 per cent. from private merchants and others. The figures for each department have been analysed in the same way. The society has three farms of its own, which supply a small proportion of the agricultural produce required. The society in its capacity of farmer is a member of the Eastern Counties Farmers' Co-operative Association. In this connection the analysis of the purchase of farm requirements is of some interest. From the C.W.S. 6·5 per cent.; from other co-operative sources (in this case the Eastern Counties), 27·8 per cent.; from private merchants, 65·7 per cent. Probably a large part of the latter item represents goods and services which neither the Eastern Counties nor C.W.S. can supply. Another department with a large percentage of non-co-operative purchases is the butchery. This indicates that the society's policy is to buy stock where possible on the farm, but failing that at markets.

The Society's Dairy Department is co-operative to a much higher degree. The percentages are: C.W.S., 57 per cent.; other co-operative sources, 16·1 per cent.; private merchants, 26·9 per cent. In the case of milk only, of which the society sells about 270,000 gallons a year, 65 per cent. is bought from the C.W.S. depot at Claydon, where it is cleaned and pasteurised, and 15 per cent. from individual farmers.

The 16 per cent. of dairy produce derived from " other co-operative sources " is probably eggs from the Framlingham Egg and Poultry Society.   This society supplies 65 to 70 per cent. of the Ipswich Society's total stock of eggs, together with small quantities of Christmas poultry, also poultry foods and appliances for use on the society's own farms, and also apparently for re-sale to the society's " back-yarder " members.   There is mutual goodwill in the relations of these two societies, emphasised by the fact that the Secretary of the Framlingham Society is (1928) President of the Ipswich Society.

The Ipswich Society has a certain number of farmer members who come in with produce of various kinds which they sell to the society, and for which the society pays in cash.   The farmers at the same time make purchases of domestic goods for which they generally require credit.

It will be observed that co-operative life in Ipswich is reaching a high degree of complexity.   An industrial society farms itself, purchases agricultural produce from individual farmers who may or may not be its own members, also from the C.W.S., some of which is once more from local farmers, and from two local farmers' organisations.   At the same time it buys farm requisites from both these farmers' societies, mostly for use on its own farms, but much also for re-sale to smallholding members.   It also sells domestic goods to farmer members who may be members of one or both of the local agricultural societies.   These societies in their turn buy farm requirements extensively from the C.W.S., and the C.W.S. buys eggs from one of them.   In the case of all these bodies at present no more than a segment of their activities thus overlap, but Ipswich (see frontispiece) gives some indication of the co-operative polity of the future, when consumers co-operation, agricultural marketing, and agricultural supply will have developed to equal strength throughout the country, and have achieved an harmonious interlocking of their functions.

A few more societies may be briefly described:

Torquay has farms of its own which are run at a profit. It tries to purchase produce direct from farmers where possible, and its vans delivering groceries in the country pick up eggs at the same time. *The South Devon Farmers Society* delivers feeding stuffs, fertilisers, etc., over the same area. The *Bruton Society* collects eggs in the same way. *Bath and Tiverton* took over an unsuccessful farmers' dairy and use it for their own milk supply. *Belfast* buys milk direct from farmers. It supervises the cleanliness, etc., of production. *Plymouth* has also a large milk business, and makes special efforts to obtain other goods direct from the farmer rather than through middlemen. The *Bristol Society* (membership in 1926, 32,064; sales, £1,006,425) buys all its milk from its own members. Many suppliers were not members when the contracts were originally made, but they have since become so, and now buy all their groceries from the society. The society also buys eggs, green stuff, etc., from farmer members, but not in sufficient quantities for its requirements. The society has only recently entered the meat business, and has not a sufficiently extensive or expert staff to buy direct, but contents itself with purchases of dead meat on the market. Farmer members of the society are also members of an agricultural society from whom they purchase requirements. *Barnsley* has organised farmers into some form of association in order to supply it with milk. *Tunbridge Wells* buys all vegetables, eggs, etc., from its own members, and this accounts for the bulk of its non-C.W.S. trade. *Runcorn* has made a special point of buying from organised farmers wherever possible.

In Ireland the only large industrial society is that of Belfast. The society does a milk trade of 45,000 gallons weekly, which is cleaned, pasteurised, and cooled by the society. The milk is derived from the society's own farm at Dundonald, and from supplying farms in counties Down, Antrim, Tyrone, Armagh, and Derry. These farms are supervised by the society to ensure the production of milk at its source under the cleanest conditions possible. The society is also understood to buy all its butter requirements from Northern Ireland co-operative creameries, the average amount being about 10 tons per week.

THE POSITION IN SCOTLAND

FROM the co-operative point of view Scotland is to a very large extent a unit and separate from England. Similar problems exist, but they are in a different stage of solution.

The industrial co-operative movement is concentrated, as is the industrial population, in the Lowlands, and especially in the neighbourhoods of Glasgow and Edinburgh. Its members and their families include an even larger percentage of the population than in England. The larger agricultural societies and those principally engaged in marketing produce, as well as supplying their members' requirements, lie around these centres of consumption. At the same time there are a great number of small societies, many of them credit societies, scattered through the remoter Highlands and islands. In this the co-operative movement merely reflects the general economic conditions of the country, which present a less complex problem than those of England.

As in England the commercial leadership of the industrial movement is concentrated in the wholesale society. The Scottish Co-operative Wholesale Society had in 1926 a trade of £16,725,948, a sum which, expressed in retail prices, would equal about 55 per cent. of the total trade of the Scottish co-operative movement. Of this about 34 per cent. represents the society's own productions, of which textile (including jute) and leather goods (£1,003,932), corn milling (£2,027,255), and preserves and pickles (£667,489), are the

activities of most interest to the agriculturist. These figures
are calculated in factory values. Of the S.C.W.S. sales to
the retail societies the following items (in wholesale prices)
are derived from farming either in Great Britain or abroad:

Tea ..	..	..	..	..	1,051,719
Sugar	..	..	..	..	1,134,020
Flour	..	..	..	..	1,743,661
Butter	..	..	..	..	1,415,191
Tobacco	..	..	..	..	542,327
Ham	..	..	..	..	584,147
Cheese	..	..	..	..	324,022
Margarine ..	..	..	..		323,022
Eggs	..	..	..	..	494,808
Oatmeal	..	..	..	..	68,573
Potatoes	..	..	..	..	230,577
			Total ..		7,912,067

The society imported from abroad in 1926 goods to the value
of £2,533,577, a very large proportion of which is from a co-
operative source. Over £2,000,000 of goods are purchased
from the English C.W.S., but it is difficult to say whether, or
to what extent, these are included amongst co-operative
imports. Tea should probably be excluded from this figure,
as it is purchased through the joint English and Scottish
Society already described, but sugar, a large portion of flour
(in its raw state as grain), tobacco, and a proportion of most
grocery goods, must be included. The S.C.W.S. has a depot
of its own in Winnipeg, from which goods to the value of
£474,607 were received in the second half of 1927. Wheat
purchases through this depot for the whole of the same year
to the value of £534,670 were derived from the Canadian
Wheat Pool. About 88 per cent. of the S.C.W.S. wheat is in
fact supplied by the Pool, and the S.C.W.S. states that,
" Unless private merchants can supply grain at a lower price

or in a more suitable position, all our purchases are made through the Pool."

The Wheat Pool has been hitherto the strongest agricultural co-operative organisation with which the S.C.W.S. has come in contact, and it was at the outset inclined to fear the strength of the Pool and its power over prices. Since then a good deal of conversation has taken place, and relations are much more cordial. The S.C.W.S. would be glad to see a closer link between the two bodies than exists at present.

The S.C.W.S. has also a grain purchasing department at Aberdeen, through which grain to the value of £28,061 was bought in the latter half of 1927. Oats to the value of £16,079 were bought in 1927 from a small number of Scottish agricultural co-operative societies. The society has also a depot at Enniskillen (Ireland) for the collection of butter (value £67,822 in 1926), eggs (£119,917), and bacon (£108,628). This represents about quarter of the society's total sale of eggs, one-fifth of bacon sales, and about one-twentieth of butter sales. A considerable proportion of these supplies is from co-operative creameries and other organisations, but it is not possible to give exact figures. Bacon to the value of £10,695, and doubtless other commodities, come from co-operative sources in Denmark. Butter is also bought from the New Zealand Produce Association, and eggs and possibly other goods from the Overseas Farmers. Eggs were also bought in fairly large quantities at one time from the United Farmers' Co-operative, Ontario, but this trade has declined largely owing to tariff changes which have discouraged the export of Canadian eggs to Europe. Eggs, cream, and butter to the value of about £10,500 were also purchased in 1927 from Scottish agricultural co-operative societies. A small amount (not much above £7,000 worth) of various agricultural produce is obtained from the S.C.W.S. own farms and gardens. The society formerly owned wheat-producing estates in Canada, but to a large extent these have been sold.

A further item of agricultural supply is cattle and dead meat which the S.C.W.S. purchased to the value of £225,851 in the latter half of 1927. It may be assumed that a very large proportion of this is home produce, and that none is at present from a co-operative source. It is in all probability bought almost entirely at Scottish markets.

The last important item of the S.C.W.S. agricultural supplies is milk. In 1926, 4,713,616 gallons were sold by the society, of which the value at wholesale prices must have been somewhere about £370,000. Until the middle of 1927 this milk was obtained direct from individual farmers, received at a number of S.C.W.S. creameries where it was cleaned and pasteurised, and thence distributed to the retail societies. In the latter half of 1927 this situation was profoundly modified by the advent of a farmers' selling organisation in the shape of the Scottish Milk Agency. This development, however, can be better discussed after a complete outline has been given of the industrial and agricultural co-operative movements.

Like the English Wholesale, the Scottish Wholesale does a certain trade with agricultural societies, chiefly in groceries and other domestic requirements. Very few of these societies are members of the S.C.W.S., though about 55 have at some time made small purchases, and 45 are recorded as having

done so in 1927. The total sales in that year amounted to
£19,842, or about one-twenty-fourth of the agricultural
societies' total purchases. This included a small sum for
feeding stuffs; but though the S.C.W.S. turn out large
quantities of offals from their mills, they have so far made
but little attempt to dispose of them in this way. The
S.C.W.S. also has customers for small amounts amongst
overseas co-operative organisations, notably agricultural
societies in Iceland.

As in England the bulk of the S.C.W.S. trade is, of course,
with the 260 retail societies which are its members. Their
sources of supply have been analysed in the last chapter,
and it is only necessary to repeat that of their total sales of
£34,500,000, rather more than half are derived from the
S.C.W.S., and of the remainder £7,000,000 are the societies'
own productions and nearly £2,000,000 those of the industrial productive societies. Both these items involve a
certain (unascertainable) basis of agricultural raw materials,
and the first includes the societies' own farms. There remains roughly £6,000,000 of goods purchased as far as is
known from private sources. A few of these societies may
transact business with local agricultural societies, but
judging from the available evidence the contract must be
small. Few appear to purchase from farmer members or even
to buy direct from farmers in general. This is not due so
much to lack of enterprise on the part of the societies as to
the general Scottish custom (a custom approved both by
buyers and sellers) of disposing of produce through a market.
The milk trade, which has enormously developed in recent
years, is an important exception which will be discussed later.

Before passing to the farmers' side of the picture, it may be worth recapitulating briefly: £34,000,000 worth of produce passes to the consumer across the counters of retail co-operative stores, perhaps four-fifths of which is of agricultural origin. Of this about £19,000,000 pass through the hands of the S.C.W.S. and £15,000,000 have passed through some form of processing, either by the S.C.W.S., the industrial productive societies, or the retail societies themselves; about £6,000,000 have not passed through co-operative hands at all. Not much more than one-ninth of the S.C.W.S. turn-over is known to be imported, but probably the amount is really higher, as this does not appear to include goods derived through England from overseas centres of production. The only items which can safely be said to be co-operative from their origin are: all liquid milk, at least one-third of the wheat purchases (Canada), a large proportion of tea, a fair quantity of home-grown oats, a proportion of butter, eggs, and bacon from Scotland, Ireland, New Zealand, and Australia (and probably also from Denmark), and a very small amount of mixed produce from the S.C.W.S. own farms.

It is now possible to turn to the goods which agricultural co-operative societies in Scotland have to put on the market, and to their general position in the national economy.

There are in Scotland 208 registered agricultural co-operative societies, with a total trade (1926) of £1,329,545. Of this, £471,025 represents the requirements sold to the societies' own members and £858,520 to the public, the items being as follows: milk and dairy produce, £727,101 (now greatly increased by the operations of the Milk Agency);

eggs and poultry, £51,761; live stock, £31,916; dead meat, £35,750; fruit and market garden produce, £2,221; sundries, £9,771 (now increased by wool sales).

All these societies are independent in a commercial sense, but all look to the leadership of the Scottish Agricultural Organisation Society, which is actively and ably exercised. Of these societies, 119 or nearly two-thirds are in the Highlands and islands, and are as a rule on a very small scale. They include nearly all the credit societies, and most of those principally concerned with poultry. General trading societies are divided almost equally between Highlands and Lowlands, but dairying (by far the most considerable single item) tends to be concentrated in the Lowlands. This distribution has undoubtedly had its effect on relations with the industrial movement.

As in England an attempt was made to secure information by means of a questionnaire. Not very much information was forthcoming, but such as it is, it throws some light on the figures of S.C.W.S. trade with agricultural societies which have already been given. Only fifty-nine replies were received. Highlands and Lowlands were represented in more or less correct proportions, but the response from poultry and dairy societies was for some reason very poor. Of these 59 societies, 9 reported that they had ceased business and 35 replied in the negative to every question; of these, 13 were Sheep Stock clubs, which are in the main credit organisations, obtaining credit through the Ministry of Agriculture; the rest are of various types, fruit, dairy, blacksmith, cattle breeding and general trading.

Fifteen societies only reported definite relations with the

industrial movement.   The proportion of these in the Highlands seems to be rather larger than the average.   Out of
fifteen of these, one is a Lowland dairy society with a fairly
large turnover which makes an annual purchase of about
£100 worth of feeding stuffs from the S.C.W.S., representing
about a quarter of its purchases.   Three are blacksmiths'
societies, two of which report purchases from co-operative
sources.   The third reports sale of blacksmith's work and
purchase of farm requirements, implements, twine and iron-
mongery to the value of £800, which represents four-fifths of
the society's turnover.   Two Sheep Stock clubs report, one the
purchase of a small quantity of seeds, the other the sale of
wool.   Of the nine general trading societies which reply
(nearly all being in the Highlands), one has ceased to do
business with the industrial movement, one buys domestic
goods to the annual value of £100, representing practically
its whole turnover; five buy both domestic and agricultural
requirements (meal and other feeding stuffs, manure, implements, etc.) to an annual value of from £200 to £3,000;
while two purchase respectively £100 and £12,000 to £15,000
a year of agricultural requirements only.   In most cases
this represents a large proportion of the total turnover of
the society in question.   Nine societies report sales to the
industrial movement; one sells £100 worth and another £350
worth of eggs to an industrial co-operative organisation, and
a third sells a small quantity of seed potatoes.   In all these
cases the figures represent practically the whole turnover of
the society.   One fruit growers' society bought suppplies at
one time from the S.C.W.S., but found the price for paper,
jute, twine, artificial manures, and spraying machines was

higher than from private merchants. This society does no
marketing, but its members sell individually to retail societies
to their mutual advantage. The report of most interest
comes from the only Egg and Poultry Society represented.
This society is a member of the local industrial society. It
purchases, in proportion to turnover, a large amount of
feeding stuffs, seeds, etc., either from the society or the
S.C.W.S., and sells a small quantity of eggs and fowls. It is
also insured for a fairly large sum with the Co-operative
Insurance Society. This is an interesting experiment in
interlocking interests, though carried out on a small scale.

The general results of the questionnaire are meagre. Undoubtedly complete returns would have shown a few more
small societies buying feeding stuffs or groceries from the
S.C.W.S., whose own figures show nearly £20,000 instead of
the £9,000 recorded, and 45 societies instead of 13, and a
considerably larger quantity of oats and other commodities
(as much as £26,509 from no more than 10 societies) passing
from agricultural co-operators to the S.C.W.S. The retail
societies, too, may be responsible for a limited amount of
inter-trading, especially in certain districts, which goes
unrecorded, but it is unlikely that the picture would be
materially altered by any fuller returns. One point only
suggests a substantial modification—namely, the fact that
milk sales in the west of Scotland are now upon a co-operative
basis.

THE MILK AGENCY.—The retail co-operative milk trade
in Scotland is a large one, and has been rapidly increasing in
recent years. Of the 280 societies affiliated to the S.C.W.S.,
60 to 70 are in the milk trade. The S.C.W.S. supplies bottled

milk to 27; it bottles 5,000 gallons daily at the society's three centres and also sells 15,000 gallons of loose milk. This milk was formerly purchased on contract from individual farmers. Early in 1927 the Scottish Agricultural Organisation Society set up a joint committee of the National Farmers' Union of Scotland and the Farmers' Co-operative Creameries, which were already federated for price-fixing purposes. It was agreed to set up a milk-selling agency, not to handle milk, but to negotiate prices and register contracts, the object being to ensure a good and stable price to the farmer. By the autumn 12 creameries and 800 individual producers guaranteeing a supply of over 40,000 gallons per day had come into the scheme; the present numbers equal 80 per cent. of the existing milk producers. The Agency charges a commission to cover the cost of its services; any surplus supplies are dealt with by the creameries which are members of the Agency. It is registered under the Industrial and Provident Societies Act. The S.C.W.S., as one of the largest milk buyers in the area covered by the Agency, was, of course, approached, as were the retail societies which do not purchase through the Wholesale. The S.C.W.S. was not at first anxious to deal with the Agency from the fear that its methods would be dictatorial (for example, it will only sell to those who deal with it exclusively), and that it would ultimately raise prices. The Wholesale, however, did not stand out long, and relations are now amicable; the Agency, as a step towards accommodation, has given the S.C.W.S. Milk Manager a seat on its board. The attitude of the retail societies has varied. Some have come in more readily than the S.C.W.S.; others still remain outside, and buy their milk direct from unorganised farmers. Amongst the latter are 4 large societies selling from 8,000 to 10,000 gallons per day. About 35 societies buy non-Agency milk, but these are not all in the area which it serves. The Agency's sales to co-operative societies amount to 28 per cent. of its total sales. It has not as yet been working long enough to show any effect in reducing the price spread between producer and consumer, as the price has not been raised to the producer nor lowered to the consumer, except by way of the dividend on purchase which is always paid by industrial societies and the dividend (bonus) on sales which may possibly be paid by the Agency if it has a surplus to dispose of. The Milk Agency is undoubtedly the most important development of inter-trading in the Scottish co-operative movements, and it is significant that the connection has come about by economic necessity and rather against than with the will of the parties concerned.

Other developments towards large scale marketing in Scotland are the Scottish Wool Growers, which has at present no links with the consumers' movement, and the newly established slaughterhouse at St. Boswells. Numerous auction marts already exist in Scotland which are frequently owned by farmers, or jointly by farmers and dealers, but which are not co-operative in character, although they promote orderly marketing. The new slaughter-house, however, will be co-operative in all respects, and may in time be able to attain a position in the meat market analogous to that of the Milk Agency in its own sphere.

Nevertheless, regarding the situation as a whole, it is clear that Scotland, with an industrial movement as well organised, and an agricultural movement probably better organised than in England, has, except in the case of milk, achieved an inconsiderable measure of inter-trading between the two movements. It must be borne in mind, of course, that there is a great disparity in size between them. The total sales of the agricultural societies in 1926 was less than 3 per cent. of that of the industrial movement, by far the larger part of this being milk and dairy produce. In that year, even supposing all their produce had been sold to the industrial movement, the agricultural societies could not have supplied more than about one-third of the dairy produce, one-tenth of the eggs, and one-third of the meat required by the S.C.W.S. alone, without taking account of the purchases of the retail societies. But the actual purchases do not amount to anything like this figure, and on each side there is a distinct " co-operative vacuum." Put in another way, there are phases of trade or production which are organised from one side or the other, but not from both. It remains to consider more closely why this should be, whether it will continue to be, and what advantages may be expected from a change.

The causes of the present situation appear to be both psychological and economic. The psychological, though powerful at the moment, are really of less importance, and as they all hang together, they may be discussed and dismissed at the outset.

The usual and inevitable opposition between the interests of producer and consumer (to be discussed more fully elsewhere) is an economic fact, and not one peculiar to Scotland. But the impress of its more obvious aspects on both producers and consumers is a psychological fact, and in the Lowlands of Scotland at least it has created a certain definite hostility between organised farmers and the consumers movement. The good fortune of the Scottish farmers co-operative movement in having a strong and efficient central organisation actively supported by the Scottish National Farmers' Union has brought inestimable advantages, but it has indirectly and involuntarily widened the breach with the industrial consumers, since Scottish societies with leaders of their own to fall back upon show less disposition than those in England—indeed, they show no disposition at all—to look to the Co-operative Wholesale Society for leadership or support. The mutual hostility has also been increased, it is difficult to say to what extent, by irrelevant political considerations, and the idea that the two movements represent respectively conservatism and socialism. The farmers, too, are undoubtedly frightened of the mere size of the industrial movement, and especially the S.C.W.S., which they suspect of using the power of its wealth and organisation to control prices to its own advantage. The industrial societies on their side are also influenced, though probably less, by a vague hostility, but even more they are indifferent to agriculture and almost ignorant of the agricultural movement. Both sides in Scotland are more purely commercial than in England, and more intolerant of the appeal to " co-operative principles." The industrialists are not inspired to evangelise the country, and the farmers do not seek an alliance with their fellow-co-operators in the towns. The extent to which the relations have been set up between the two movements is, therefore, all the more remarkable and the more indicative of their economic value.

Turning to the economic situation it must be remembered,

as has been noted before, that the marketing of produce is, on the whole, better organised in Scotland. It usually passes from producer to retailer with no intervening party but the auctioneer. The ordinary middleman only exists for the small retailer who cannot himself purchase economically in the market. There is also a good sale for produce both locally and, in the case of meat, in England. The farmer is fairly prosperous, or at least thinks himself so; he has not felt the pinch or been driven to special measures in the way of marketing. On the other hand, the marketing system is probably not perfect; it is true, for instance, that grain is frequently sold by farmers to middlemen for re-sale to other farmers. The effect of these conditions on the industrial movement is that they in their turn purchase home produce very largely in the market rather than straight from the farm, as an enterprising co-operative society will do in England. This again removes them further from any personal contact with the farmer. Buying on the market is a simple process, and it can be done in bulk, but the produce of farmers' co-operative societies has to be picked up in relatively small quantities and is sometimes insufficiently graded. Managers of industrial societies or even of the S.C.W.S. departments have as a rule very little idea of what is actually being offered for sale by agricultural societies. These conditions apply especially to the Highlands, where the majority of societies are situated, and where the absence of markets would otherwise be favourable to direct sales. The uncertainties of transport in remote districts also impede relations.

The industrial movement wants produce in bulk and

graded, at least up to a point.   On the other hand, if a society undertake very high grading of a semi-luxury commodity like eggs, it may find it is only repaid by taking the additional trouble necessary to sell its produce in small parcels to hotels and similar consumers.   Another objection to inter-trading sometimes heard is that the two movements, even together, are not large enough to dominate the market, and as soon as any alliance between them becomes known, under-cutting by the private merchant is accelerated.   This, of course, may have its advantages for both sides, but it does not lead to stability or permanent relations.

The sales from the S.C.W.S. to agricultural societies is a distinct problem, and in some ways a simpler one.   As it is, about 4 per cent. of the requirements purchased by agricultural societies for their members' use are from the S.C.W.S., and practically the whole of this represents domestic goods. At the same time the S.C.W.S. owns large flour mills, and turns out great quantities of offals suitable for feeding stuffs. This position is obviously irrational.   The farmers' societies appear satisfied with private supplies.   The industrial movement, on the other hand, has probably given less thought to this subject than has been given in England.   Their approach to agriculture is still more or less haphazard.   The S.C.W.S. has no special agricultural department.   Although the by-products of its mills are available for sale to farmers' societies, the trade has not been developed, and methods of salesmanship, etc., have not been sufficiently adapted to agricultural peculiarities.   Further, the farmers' society has a tendency to demand longer credit than the S.C.W.S. is prepared to give. The S.C.W.S. is reported to sell at a higher price than other merchants, though it is probable this is neutralised by the dividend on purchase. Again, the S.C.W.S. prefers to sell immediately and in large quantities rather than store its by-products and subsequently sell them in small quantities to a number of small scattered societies. Hence the S.C.W.S. sells the bulk of its millers' offals to private wholesalers who not infrequently retail them to farmers' co-operative societies. Where the S.C.W.S. trades at all with a farmers' society, it tends to be the sole supplier or purchaser. Such cases are largely amongst the small Highland societies. The reason is possibly to some extent that these societies have not come into direct opposition to the industrial movement, and therefore do not regard it with any hostility. Insofar as they sell domestic goods they are, of course, indistinguishable from industrial societies themselves. Highland societies, too, tend to take the idealist view of co-operation. It is also possible that they are less well catered for by other wholesalers.

The conclusions seem to be: (1) that there is room for a great increase both in the sale of farm produce to the industrial movement, and the purchase of farm requirements from it; (2) that there is no enthusiasm or even conscious intention towards this development on either side; (3) that nevertheless there is a purely economic trend towards it which is freely admitted by the responsible leaders on both sides; (4) that the greatest step forward will be the building up of the producers' organisation till it is of equal service and strength with that of the consumers.

INTER-RELATIONS ABROAD

THE general characteristics of inter-relations abroad which distinguish them from those existing within and between British countries are, firstly, that they are relatively small; secondly, that they tend to be between local societies rather than national bodies; and, thirdly, that these relations tend to be organic and their co-operative character is in most cases highly developed.

The consumers' movement itself differs considerably from the British model. In many countries it is predominantly rural, and resembles nothing in Britain except the small societies in Wales and the Highlands of Scotland, which deal principally in groceries, and to a lesser extent in agricultural requirements. Foreign societies of this type, however, are frequently important and highly successful bodies. A consequence of this situation is that, amongst relatively backward peasants especially, the demand for agricultural produce in co-operative stores is small, as the population is almost self-supporting in the matter of food. This means that the co-operative store stocks principally clothing, hardware, and tropical produce, and that the agricultural producer exports his produce occasionally, as in the U.S.S.R., through the consumers' society, but more often through a specialised marketing society.

The relatively small scale of inter-relations is to some extent caused by this circumstance, as is the smallness of co-operative imports. On the whole, the consumers' move-ment in peasant countries handles the type of produce least likely to be co-operative at the source. The continental movements are probably less strongly centralised than the British movement, which is a factor in the situation tending to make all contacts local, but the prevalence and success of these contacts is probably due to the vitality and nearly equal strength of both movements. This, it would appear, has led them to substitute in many cases genuinely co-operative machinery for simple commercial transactions.

Milk is one of the commodities which have been dealt with most successfully, and the systems in force in societies in Czechoslovakia, France, and the U.S.A., are all worthy of study. The more elaborate and comprehensive Hungarian schemes are also extremely interesting. A principle of the greatest importance has been applied in one or two instances and deserves further emphasis. This is the payment of dividend by the same body on co-operative sales and co-operative purchases. In the Czechoslovakian dairy men-tioned below, and in the British joint organisations all profits are divided according to share-holdings. But in the U.S.A. society the profits of a special department and in the Swedish societies, the surplus on all transactions is distributed as dividend on purchases from, as well as sales to, members. It is extremely difficult to distribute this kind of social wealth in strict proportion to the share each member has had in creating it, and a logical division is further impeded by the purchases from non-members which are bound to be made by a consumers' society. Nevertheless, the American and Swedish solution would seem to be satisfactory for all practical purposes, and is undoubtedly most in accord with co-operative principles.

Inter-relations between co-operative organisations abroad have been the subject of research by the International Labour Office and the International Institute of Agriculture in Rome. Both bodies have issued reports, to which the reader is referred for detailed information on various continental undertakings. The following pages contain a summary of the position in all the principal countries.

AUSTRIA

The Consumers' Wholesale Society imports agricultural produce from the Russian Co-operative Societies through a joint company " The Ratao," similar in form to the Anglo-Russian Grain Export Company (see Chapter V.), and exports manufactured produce in return.

Butter is purchased by the industrial societies to a considerable extent direct from farmers' co-operative marketing associations. The proportions are as follows: 62 per cent. from marketing associations, 35 per cent. from farmers, and the rest from the Wholesale Society.

BELGIUM

The Belgian industrial movement has always been closely associated with the Social Democratic Party, and its first efforts to extend the movement into the country were, to a large extent, a form of political penetration. In 1897 a few branches of industrial societies had been established in the country, together with one dairy. At this time the Boerenbond or Peasants' Union was established under clerical influence. This has now 112,978 members, and is principally engaged in the supply of requirements. Marketing is not carried on to any great extent, as markets are readily available. The sectarian divergence has probably helped to keep the two movements apart. In 1904 the Congress of the Consumers' Movement passed a resolution instructing societies to organise the sale of agricultural produce, and to establish central dairies. At the Congress of 1922 the extension of branches into the country was advocated, also the establishment of a central buying agency. The latter proposal has not so far been carried out. The consumers' movement imports a small quantity of goods from abroad, and one of its most active and successful societies—that of Liège—buys grain from its members who are farmers.

BULGARIA

Co-operative bazaars have been jointly organised by producers and consumers' co-operative societies, but no details of their constitution or methods of operating are available.

CZECHOSLOVAKIA

A joint society of co-operative milk producers and consumers exists in Moravia. Half the capital was contributed by the producers' organisations, and the other half jointly by consumers' co-operative societies and municipalities. The producers appoint five directors, and the consumers four; the chairman is a representative of the producers. In accordance with Czechoslovakian law and custom, a supervisory council is also appointed, in which the proportion of representation is reversed. The dairy can deal with 30,000 litres daily, though in 1925 consumption had not reached this point. The dairy also makes cheese, doubtless from surplus. Shareholders who are producers hand over their whole supply of milk to the dairy, and consumer shareholders agree to buy their entire requirements from it. Both the purchasing and the selling price is fixed in accordance with market rates, with an addition for butter fat content. No remarkable decrease in price spread has occurred, the object of the society having been rather to secure a regular market on the one hand, and good and regular supplies on the other.

There is also a co-operative warehousing society for the sale of cereals, which has a large mill and contracts for the sale of flour to co-operative bakeries. It has drawn up model contracts, which have been used for a large number of similar trading relations. One or two consumers' societies with a large rural membership own flour mills and draw supplies of grain from peasants. They do not, however, pay any dividend on produce sold to the society. Societies of this type sell agricultural requirements as well as domestic goods. Relations between producers and consumers are not equally cordial in all parts of the country, but efforts are being made to improve them.

DENMARK

Danish industrial co-operation is at present a much less considerable movement than the agricultural organisation. Close relations exist between the Consumers' Wholesale and certain specialised branches of agricultural co-operation. For example, the Co-operative Wholesale Society participates in the control of the Seed Production Co-operative in its functions as distributor to consumers' co-operative societies.

FRANCE

The Fédération Nationale des Sociétés de Consommation and the Fédération des Sociétés Agricoles et Mutualistes have for some time been seeking means of collaboration. Various early attempts to establish inter-relations were described in Chapter II. In 1922 a permanent Joint Committee was set up. A Bill was brought before Parliament establishing mixed organisations of producers and consumers which would be eligible as recipients of long-term credit. The French industrial movement imports goods of co-operative origin to a limited amount including (1926) 20,000 kilograms of Greek currents.

Various local societies have combined functions as producers and consumers. Rural bakeries receive members' corn, grind, and bake it, and return it to them in the form of bread. Wine-growers' co-operative societies make soap from grape pips which they return to members, and cheese societies also return a part of their products to suppliers of milk.

The milk business supplies some good examples of local inter-trading. The Union of Paris Industrial Societies obtains its milk supplies, as far as is possible, from agricultural societies. A detailed scheme has been worked out in Lorraine; in 1924 an agreement was concluded between the Lorraine Co-operative Union and the Dairy of St. Aubin sur Aire, by which the dairy bound itself to send all its milk, pasteurised, to the Co-operative Union, and the Union bound itself to accept all milk supplied. The price was to be fixed in accordance with market rates, with a deduction of 10 per cent. to cover the Union's costs of handling. Butter was to be forwarded in the same way, and similar arrangements were made for eggs.

FINLAND

Considerable competition has taken place between dairies carried on by co-operative producers and co-operative consumers. Nevertheless, considerable inter-trading takes place. One of the two principal industrial co-operative unions buys 78 per cent. of its butter and 25 per cent. of its cheese from agricultural co-operative societies. The consumers' co-operative movement imports co-operative goods to the value of £30,320 from abroad. It has a large rural membership, but agricultural co-operative production is largely for export.

ESTHONIA

The Esthonian co-operative movement imports co-operative goods to the value of £27,972 from abroad.

GERMANY

The German industrial societies have for some time past aimed at buying direct from growers and growers co-operative societies. The difficulties in the way of carrying out such a policy have been partly political—the peasants objecting to the social democratic character of the industrial movement—but to a greater extent economic. Perhaps the greatest of all have been those connected with commercial custom. The peasants had been in the habit of selling to dealers who came to their doors, and co-operative marketing, as distinct from co-operative purchase of requirements, was little developed amongst them. The managers of industrial co-operative societies, on the other hand, were accustomed to sit in their offices and await the coming of travellers anxious to sell goods. Extensive inter-trading did not begin till both sides had extended from local branches to federations. In the meantime some progress was made. From 1904 the German movement obtained about 5 per cent. of its agricultural produce direct from growers or growers' co-operative societies. (This did not amount to more than 1 per cent. of its total turnover.) Included in this were imports from the co-operative societies of Finland and Siberia. The War and the rationing system put an end to this development, but the trade was afterwards gradually resumed. At first, growers were hostile, but later they were eager to expand trade with the co-operative movement as a check on middlemen's prices. In 1922 a joint conference was held and a joint committee, the " Economic Council of German Co-operative Productive and Distributive Societies " was formed, of which the four largest co-operative unions in Germany are members. The objects of the Council were stated as follows:

" The principal unions for the organisations for production and distribution bind themselves to promote, in so far as in them lies, the practice of the direct purchase of food-stuffs by the co-operative stores from the agricultural societies."

This Committee has not at present achieved any marked results, except in the handling of potatoes. Milk is also the subject of direct trade.

In 1920 the German (Consumers') Wholesale Society imported from foreign co-operative societies or depots abroad goods to the value of £319,044. In 1925 it imported 1,471,000 eggs from co-operative sources.

One or two local experiments of some interest have been carried out, amongst them the foundation of the joint society " Town and Country " in Freiburg. The agricultural productive societies joining the organisation may either have direct dealings with the industrial societies or may set up a central agency. The two parties contribute equal capital to the joint organisation and have equal rights and duties. A joint fruit and vegetable market has been set up by societies on both sides.

HUNGARY

The position here is somewhat unusual, but extremely interesting. The Co-operative Wholesale Society, Hangya, is the centre of a group of societies, 90 per cent. of whose members are farmers. It is engaged both in the marketing of agricultural produce and in retail distributive trade in foodstuffs to its relatively small urban membership, and in manufactured articles to the rural population. It controls a limited company (all shares being held either by Hangya itself or its members) which manufactures domestic and chemical goods and mills flour. These goods are intended primarily for co-operative distribution, but the manufacturing company can also sell on the open market.

The Hangya and the Central Co-operative Credit Society between them have also established a separate limited company, the Futura, for large-scale marketing of grain, wool, and feathers sent in by the affiliated societies of both organisations.   These goods are for the most part exported, as a better price can be obtained abroad.   Thus the co-operative flour mill owned by Hangya is by no means certain of obtaining grain from the Futura, half of whose shares are also held by Hangya, and in fact usually purchases direct from the farmers.   This is a defect in an otherwise valuable experiment.

ITALY

No relations between co-operative societies have been traced, though the farmers' societies are known to sell dairy produce and rice direct to the consumer.

LATVIA

The co-operative movement in Latvia is a post-war development, and has been very successful.   The consumers' movement is principally rural, and does not deal largely in foodstuffs, as its members live off their farms.   Its principal trade is in household goods and agricultural requirements. It imports a small quantity of goods from foreign co-operative sources.   The individual farmer-members of consumers' societies sell their produce to their societies to a limited extent, but there are also farmers' marketing societies principally engaged in exporting.

NORWAY

An organisation exists for the disposal of peasants' produce by agreement between the Consumers' Co-operative Federation and the Peasants' and Smallholders' Union. The consumers' movement also imports a small quantity of foreign co-operative produce.

The Scandinavian Co-operative Wholesale Society is a Federation of the Wholesales of Sweden, Norway, and Denmark, principally engaged in importing. In 1925 its imports valued £1,061,000, of which £160,000 represented wheat and flour from the U.S.A.

POLAND

The question of overlapping between agricultural and consumers' societies was made the subject of a detailed agreement in 1923. The imports from foreign co-operative sources in 1925 was £81,578.

SWEDEN

In the north of Sweden a strong farmers' movement exists in connection with the consumers' movement. Farmers are members of the consumers' societies, and sell produce, especially milk, direct to them. Butter is manufactured in creameries owned by the societies. The farmers in return draw manufactured goods and imported food from the societies. They receive dividend both on sales and purchases. The societies also arrange for the purchase of machinery on behalf of the farmers.

In the south, milk distribution is frequently undertaken by farmers' co-operative societies. The Stockholm consumers' society has contracted to obtain all its milk supplies from the farmers' society of the district, which also sells to the Stockholm public generally. The consumers' movement buys all its butter from the farmers' societies, but its cheese is purchased in the market. The imports of the Swedish consumers' movement from co-operative sources amounted to £12,447 in 1925.

SWITZERLAND

Inter-trading in Switzerland is carried on almost entirely in dairy produce. In milk distribution, competition has occurred between framers' societies and consumers' societies, where both have engaged in retailing, and this has been especially acute in Basle. As in England, consumers' societies not infrequently own farms. The position, however, has recently improved. In Geneva the Agricultural Milk Producers Association has concluded a ten-years' contract to supply the consumers' society with two-thirds of its requirements, the price being fixed so as to enable the society to cover the costs of distribution. The consumers' society of Chaux de Fonds has a large rural membership, and buys all its milk from the Milk Producers' Association. It contracts to take the full output of the Association's members, and converts surplus into cheese. In Basle and Zurich the Milk Producers' Association supplies milk to dairies, half-yearly contracts being made on terms drawn up by the Central Federation of Swiss Milk Producers.

Practically all the export of cheese is in the hands of the Union of the Swiss Cheese Trade, a body which includes two private companies, three farmers' co-operative societies, and the Swiss Union of Consumers' Societies.

The Swiss consumers' movement buys all cheese from farmers' producing societies. It also imports (1926) goods to the value of £25,402 from co-operative societies abroad. Its general imports for the same year included 1,412 tons of butter, of which 1,111 tons were direct from co-operative producers in Denmark.

United States of America[1]

Consumers' co-operation in the U.S.A. is still a small development as compared with the agricultural movement, and in this the position resembles that in the British Dominions. In 1925 there were 1,703 consumers' societies; half of these included farmers amongst their members, and some, especially in the Middle West, had an entirely agricultural membership.

In 1926 the Congress of the Consumers' League passed a resolution advocating direct relations between co-operative producers and consumers, and set up a committee to study the problem.

Various instances of inter-trading between local societies may be given. The Wenatchee Farmer-Labor Exchange marketed its first co-operative apple crop through a consumers' store. A milk producers' society in Minnesota, with 6,000 members, supplies milk to the Franklin Co-operative Creamery, a flourishing consumers' organisation supplying 30,000 families. In 1924 the sales of milk and dairy produce valued $3,000,000. By eliminating the middleman, these societies have reduced the retail price to the consumer, and at the same time raised the price paid to the farmer. The Waukegan Consumers' Society (Illinois) also carries on a milk business. It contracted with farmers that those who supplied milk should subscribe sufficient capital to the society to cover investment in the dairy, and that the society should guarantee a satisfactory basic price for milk. In consequence of this arrangement, the farmers have re-

---

[1] See also chapter on Empire Production.

ceived an improved price for their milk. All profits of the dairy department are returned to producers and consumers in proportion to the price received by the producers and the price paid by the consumers for the milk.

UNION OF SOCIALIST SOVIET REPUBLICS[1]

The Consumers' Co-operative Movement in the U.S.S.R. includes both peasants and industrial workers, and aims consciously at uniting their interests. Even in rural districts it is stronger than the agricultural producers' movement, which, though increasing, is not at present capable of feeding the co-operative population of the towns. The central organ of the consumers' movement is Centrosojus, which is both Union and Wholesale Society, and buys both agricultural produce and manufactured articles for its member-societies. The consumers' societies are independent buyers of agricultural produce, principally grain, butter, eggs, flax and furs. Raw materials are, for the most part, exported. In 1926-27 the sales of rural co-operative societies of all kinds was £175,585,000, of which 17 per cent. was agricultural produce sold by the peasants to the towns. The bulk of this was grain, which passed into the hands of the urban co-operative societies, and some of which was exported. In some cases this was doubtless collected by the consumers' societies from their peasant members, in others purchased by them from farmers' marketing societies, while in some cases the farmers' societies themselves controlled all sales.

In 1927 the consumers' societies purchased by special agreement 25 per cent. of their grain, 50 per cent. of their

[1] See also chapters on Empire Production and Joint Undertakings.

butter, and 18 per cent. of their eggs from peasants' marketing societies. An arrangement was made to prevent overlapping through the consumers' organisation buying from individual peasants rather than their societies. There is not, however, a very large sale of agricultural produce through the consumers' movement, as its peasant members not only supply themselves, but tend to sell perishables direct to urban consumers in the markets. It is especially hoped to organise fully the handling of grain, butter, and meat, and the establishment of a joint meat organisation is being considered. The consumers' movement has its own fisheries, and also handles a large quantity of fish from other sources; the Centrosojus and its member-societies have their own productive works for soap, tobacco, boots, canned goods, tea, cocoa, and coffee. They are large flour millers. Further development and systematisation of the relations between producers and consumers are under discussion. A good deal of local interchange takes place in organisational as well as commercial spheres, and experiments have been made in the appointment of agricultural representatives to the boards of consumers' societies and vice versa. Another development is the policy of handing over the exports of raw materials and foodstuffs to the producers' organisations. The whole question of the foreign relations of the Russian co-operative movements has been discussed in previous chapters.

CONCLUSIONS

Iт remains to sum up the position as regards inter-trading, to discuss its advantages and disadvantages, and the probability or the reverse of its extension in future.

It has been shown in the foregoing chapters how streams of co-operative produce flow from most of the Dominions and many other countries to Great Britain, and how a part of this supply finds its way into the reservoir of the Co-operative Wholesale Society, whence it is dispersed to the retail co-operative societies and through them to the individual consumer. It has been shown also how the C.W.S. here and there makes a return in goods or services to the exporting organisations, and how joint organisations have been set up between them. Further, it has been explained how the same conditions are reproduced on a national scale in Great Britain with the difference that the C.W.S. sales of requirements to agricultural societies exceed in importance their purchases of produce, while the whole trade is upon a smaller scale. Finally, the local inter-relations of industrial and agricultural societies have been described, and consideration given to the relevant questions of policy and principle which have occupied the minds of co-operators for the past sixty years.

The subject has two main aspects based on the agricultural society's two principal functions: (1) the supply of requirements; and (2) the marketing of produce. The first, so far as inter-trading is concerned, mainly affects Great Britain; the subject is full of complicated details and is best treated first.

The farmers' society supplying feeding stuffs does not differ economically from the industrial society supplying groceries. Both are organisations of consumers. Such a society is just as much in need of a wholesale organisation at its back to bulk its orders and secure the full benefit of combination. If it can share the wholesale machinery set up by the industrial societies, so much the better; it will save overhead charges and obviate the friction which might, and in time past did, arise between two bodies with similar functions. But the advantages do not stop here. The agricultural requirements that bulk largest in the farmers' orders—feeding stuffs and manures—are all the by-products of some industrial process. The Co-operative Wholesale Society of the Industrial Movement carries on these processes, and has the farmers' requirements to dispose of without the trouble and expense of purchasing them in the market as any non-manufacturing wholesale agency would need to do.

But here a curious element in the situation must be pointed out. The fundamental principle of the consumers' co-operative movement is production for use and not for profit. But the C.W.S. finds such things as millers' offals on its hands whether it wants them or not. As a by-product they are not produced in accordance with any demand; the C.W.S. must dispose of them whether there is a co-operative call for them or not. The supply, price, and so on, of commodities of this type are really controlled by two sets of consumers—the price of offals, for instance, not only by the consumers of offals but by the consumers of flour, and in the co-operative movement to-day, and still more in the past, the consumption of flour tends to be larger and better organised than the consumption of offals.

At first the C.W.S. attempted rather to dispose of certain inevitable by-products, than to create a co-operative service for agriculturists. But as co-operative organisation of farmers progressed, the C.W.S. widened its aims, and its agricultural department now caters fairly completely for the farmers needs. It must be borne in mind, of course, that the C.W.S. is a democratic organisation controlled ultimately by men with an industrial outlook, so that certain slowness in understanding the farmer's point of view is not unnatural. The general consensus of opinion amongst farmers' societies is that the quality of C.W.S. supplies is good, though it is not infrequently added that the price is high. The high price, however, is sometimes held to be neutralised by the dividend on purchase. There are developments still to be made in the direction of more extensive supplies of machinery and foreign feeding stuffs. Such things obviously would have to be bought or manufactured by the C.W.S. with the express object of sale to agriculturists; the progress that has been made in this direction marks a departure from the position of the farmer simply as a consumer of by-products.

That is the trend of development, and it seems clearly in the interests of farmers' societies to forward it, and to encourage the growth of a section of the C.W.S. which will be completely at their service. They do can this by trading with the C.W.S., and, as many have done already, by taking shares in it and becoming affiliated members. Membership entitles them to vote at quarterly meetings, and to receive the full dividend of 3d. in the £ on their purchases. But there are many cases in which this apparently natural and useful course of action has not been taken, and it is well to state the reasons:

1. *Lack of Information.*—Some of the smaller and remoter societies have never heard of the C.W.S. at all, or do not know how it differs from any other provender merchant.

2. *Unsuitability of Supplies or Prices.*—Some societies have sampled C.W.S. supplies, and have found them higher in price than others they can obtain, or their members' taste runs to some particular brand of cake, etc., which the C.W.S. does not supply. This is an ordinary commercial obstacle, which has nothing to do with co-operation.

3. *Distrust.*—The liquidation of the Agricultural Wholesale Society and the resultant losses to farmers' societies has inspired many with a fear of allying themselves with any co-operative wholesale organisation.

4. *Hostility.*—This is a vague psychological phenomenon which is probably of diminishing importance, but is none the less worth analysing. It seems to be made up of various elements.

(*a*) The C.W.S. is known to be a " consumers' organisation," and the farmer, as a producer, feels it must be really working against his interests. Also he associates it, quite correctly, with the local industrial society which he may consider is trying to reduce the price of agricultural produce.

(*b*) The C.W.S. presents itself to the farmer as a colossal impersonal trust contrasted with his own small business, or comparatively small co-operative society, and he is afraid of its power.

(c) The Industrial Movement is a working-class movement, associated with increased wages and similar developments which the farmer considers to be directed against himself.

(d) The Industrial Movement is associated with the Labour Movement, and the farmer is generally a Conservative.

(e) The C.W.S. is itself a purchaser of agricultural produce, and the farmer may have come into contact with it directly or through this society, and have felt that the bargain was a hard one. This is a real objection, and will be discussed further.

(f) The farmers' society may have actually experienced the jealousy or hostility of a local industrial society. Curiously enough, however, this perfectly genuine injury seems to have occasioned less annoyance than regret amongst the farmers' societies who have been subject to it. The whole matter, however, is part of the difficult question of overlapping, which will be discussed later.

Briefly, it may be said that (a) is based on an economic misconception, for the functions of the C.W.S. as consumers' wholesale are perfectly compatible with its functions as farmers' provider; (b) is remedied by the farmers' societies becoming themselves part of the trust they fear and deriving strength from it; (c) and (d) are mainly matters of opinion or sentiment, as neither point is likely to affect the business policy of the C.W.S.; and (e) and (f) are genuine, but not insuperable difficulties.

Hostility to retail industrial societies is sometimes greater

than to the C.W.S., because they are felt to be consumers
exclusively; sometimes less, because they are more equal in
strength with the agricultural society.

5. *Overlapping.*—This takes place in various ways, but
it always means that one party has had the enterprise, the
luck, or, in some cases, merely the rashness, to push its
undertakings across what the other considers to be the proper
producer-consumer frontier, and that a duplication of
services, sometimes complicated by undercutting, has
resulted. Sometimes there is no duplication, for the stronger
movement has simply appropriated functions which in other
circumstances might have been exercised by its rival, and the
usurpation may not even have given offence. The following
are the main types of overlapping:

(*a*) The industrial society has an agricultural department,
and sells feeding stuffs, etc., in competition with the farmers'
society.

(*b*) The industrial and agricultural societies both have
milk rounds, or the agricultural society wholesales milk, or
its members sell milk individually in competition with the
industrial society.

(*c*) The agricultural society sells groceries to its members
in competition with an industrial society in the same district.

(*d*) The industrial society opens a shop for the sale of
fruit, dairy produce, etc., to the general public, which com-
petes in the same way.

All these problems are difficult of solution; perhaps it is an
advantage that in very few is it possible to say that either
party is morally wrong or right. Every case is a matter for
negotiation and, it would seem, for the services of some sort

of conciliation board. Point (*a*) would appear the most serious cause of friction, for in cases where an industrial society was first in the field and a farmers' society was subsequently formed to deal with the same commodities, the jealousy of the industrial society is often sufficient to exclude the agricultural society from membership of the C.W.S. Generally speaking, it would seem that where there is any danger of overlapping, retail societies should not handle farm requirements, nor agricultural societies articles of human consumption, and that both should agree to hand over to one another any customers for these articles. This, however, is too cut and dried a solution to be applicable unmodified; the individual cases are bound to be highly complex.

On the C.W.S. side only one serious objection seems to be entertained to trading with farmers' societies—namely, that credit is required by farmers to a degree which appears startling to men trained in the traditions of the industrial movement.

It is sometimes debated whether or not farmers' societies should confine their purchasing to the C.W.S. In so far as the C.W.S. agricultural department is their own, controlled by their votes and adapted to their needs, loyalty to it is undoubtedly economically desirable. Even so, the department is none the worse because its customers are on the alert to see that it is actually selling the best goods at the lowest possible prices. But it must be borne in mind that at present the policy of the agricultural department is also influenced by the requirements of the industrial societies who form the great majority of C.W.S. members, and that farmers' societies, if they cannot by their votes secure a preponderant voice in the affairs of their department, may influence it by their power to purchase or to abstain from purchasing. Many farmers' societies which have the strongest sense of the value to them of the C.W.S. do not hesitate to purchase elsewhere when need arises.

Linked with the question of supply of requirements by the C.W.S. is that of its general services to the agricultural society—banking and insurance, auditing, advice, supervision in cases where the agricultural society has got into difficulties. The C.W.S. bank has been valuable to the industrial societies, and also to a number of agricultural societies. In the case of the Westralian Farmers, Ltd., it has provided credit on more advantageous terms than private banks. Neither its activities nor those of the insurance department call for any special comment, nor are they the subject of any controversy.

The usefulness of the C.W.S. advisory and supervisory services to the agricultural societies is a point on which there is somewhat more division of opinion. It has been urged, for instance, that dependence on the C.W.S. saps the self-reliance of agricultural societies. It may be objected, however, that to take advantage of the business experience of the C.W.S. officials is not necessarily to become dependent on the C.W.S., and that a capable manager will take any advice or support he can get without surrendering his freedom of action. Also, it has been abundantly shown that a considerable number of societies have been saved from extinction by the timely aid of the C.W.S. In a number of cases the C.W.S. undertakes the auditing of societies' accounts; the industrial societies have for many years found this system work to their advantage.

The question of the sales of produce by the agricultural to the industrial movement raises a very different set of considerations. Here, there are no attractions of membership, control, or dividend to encourage inter-trading, no utilisation of by-products, no community of interest between one type of consumer and another. Agricultural producers anxious to sell dear are confronted by industrial consumers anxious to buy cheap, and it may well be asked what reason they have to trade with one another rather than with anyone else on the market. Upon which it may be further asked to what extent inter-trading is deliberate at all and not merely fortuitous contact which every considerable seller is likely at some time or other to make with every considerable buyer.

Before trying to decide these questions it will be well to look more closely into the facts of the case. A number of English agricultural societies have certainly entertained at one time or another the idea that they should receive better terms from any organisation acting under the co-operative name than from a private firm. At the same time a number of industrial societies have of deliberate purpose set out to buy their supplies from farmers' organisations. It is usually a certain satisfaction to any organisation to deal with a body organised on the same principles as itself. Both attempts have succeeded in some places, failed in others. Where they have been persisted in, it is because they have been, in time at least, a commercial success. Where they have not been a commercial success they have invariably been dropped. On the other hand, a number of relationships have been entered into without deliberate purpose which have likewise proved commercially advantageous to both parties. From one cause or another intertrade has grown from nothing to a very considerable volume of business.

It will be convenient here to sum up the factors which have contributed both to the frequent successes and the occasional failures.

The industrial movement is a satisfactory buyer of agricultural produce, because its orders are large and regular, and because it pays regularly, promptly, and with certainty. It also buys a good quality article, and from the point of view of the British farmer it is an advantage that co-operative taste prefers home produce.[1] It will also in some instances buy produce on commission, disposing on the market of what it does not itself require, though how far this meets agricultural requirements it is difficult to say. It understands the value of graded produce.

On the other hand, the industrial movement wishes, like all other buyers, to buy cheap. It buys in bulk, and expects a corresponding reduction in price. It has a working-class membership, and cannot sell expensive produce. It has to face the competition of other retailers. It is in a strong commercial position, and can draw supplies from a variety of sources. Where the industrial movement can buy from the source—that is, the individual farmer—it will sometimes

[1] According to Co-operative managers, only 30 per cent. of the meat consumed by the co-operative public is imported, as compared with 60 per cent. in the case of the whole population.

regard the agricultural society in the light of an unnecessary middleman, although the utility of producers' marketing societies is officially endorsed by the C.W.S. On the other hand, the C.W.S. sometimes insists that an agricultural society shall not sell direct to an industrial society, but that all produce should be sold through its own agency.

It may be said that, on the whole, from the point of view of the agricultural society, the advantages of inter-trading predominates over the disadvantages. No agricultural society is likely to trade exclusively with the industrial movement, unless its knowledge of what is going on in the outside market assures it that it is doing so with advantage. But there are cases where an agricultural society will find it worth while to use its powers of grading and organisation, and the time and labour at its disposal, to sell to more advantage in small quantities on a luxury market.

The question of co-operative agencies and middlemen seems to be one for reconsideration. The feeling on the agricultural side is that if the C.W.S. wishes to act as agent for all its affiliated societies and claims that the system makes for efficiency, the agricultural society should in the same way act as agent for its members.

Looking at the question of inter-trading from the point of view of the industrial society, it can be observed that the factor of co-operative policy or principles does undoubtedly enter into the considerations making for inter-trading, though this is sometimes more the case with management committees or directors who have been chosen for their general knowledge of co-operation, than with buyers who have been chosen for their commercial abilities. Nevertheless, there is a widespread feeling that the farmer must receive fair play, that he has not always done so, and that he should be encouraged to improve his position by organisation. Also that the industrial society should be ready to agree to a slight rise in farmers' prices where it can do so without injury to itself from its competitors.

Turning to practical considerations, the industrial society saves time and labour in buying from the agricultural society rather than from the individual farmer, provided that the agricultural society can dispose of reasonably large quantities of produce of a quality which is uniform and reaches the required standard—regular supply, regular delivery of standard grade, and uniform packing and preparation, being the outstanding requirements. It must be remembered, however, that in the present inadequate state of agricultural co-operation it is easier to buy on a market or from a wholesale merchant, and that the price may not be higher. The advantages of grading are probably lost, together with the stable and non-speculative character of co-operative marketing; nevertheless, in the present circumstances of the British agricultural movement, the industrial society, wholesale or retail, once it has got behind the private wholesaler, tends, as has been indicated, to go straight to the individual farmer. The C.W.S. as a provender merchant is anxious to secure the custom of agricultural societies, however small, but as a purchaser it has no special commercial motive for seeking a connection. The same thing applies even more to the retail industrial societies who are purchasers and purchasers only. They can always buy elsewhere, and they are not inconvenienced if no inter-- relations exist.

This indifference ceases wherever agricultural co-operation is anything like equal in strength to the industrial movement, and the agricultural societies, as in the case of those in the Dominions and abroad, have a really strong position on the market and the efficiency that accompanies and conditions large-scale undertakings. This position may even be so strong that the British situation is reversed and the industrial movement feels itself in turn becoming subservient to a more powerful organisation. This temporary outstripping of one movement by another is inevitable and by no means unhealthy. The main point is that the growth in inter- relations is brought about more than by anything else simply by the growth of the farmers' organisation. The larger both organisations are, the more they are bound to meet one another and the more mutually beneficial their relations will be. Minor obstacles will tend to disappear, and the efficiency of both sides will increase.

Two forms of inter-relations which are at present of minor importance may be briefly recalled. A few industrial societies hold shares in agricultural societies. This differs from financial operations such as the C.W.S. financing of the Wheat Pool in Western Australia, from the fact that the connection is permanent and unconnected with the marketing of any particular crop. In some cases an industrial society holding shares in an agricultural society receives dividend on any agricultural produce it may purchase. This form of relationship already exists extensively in England between the industrial consumers' societies and the industrial productive societies engaged in boot-making, printing, and textile trades, etc.

The Co-operative Union—the educational and propagandist centre of the industrial movement—is open to membership of the agricultural societies, and is anxious to welcome them to its ranks. A few societies have already joined, but the vast majority of its members are still industrial organisations. At the same time, the Union has reappointed an Agricultural Committee, and is endeavouring to frame a policy which will be of real value to the agricultural movement. The Union has no commercial functions, but the inducement held out for agricultural societies to become members is that they may thereby help to develop the rural side of this influential body. It provides a common meeting-place where their point of view may be advanced and explained, where the problems and difficulties of inter-relations may be discussed.

It has been asked how far inter-trading is desirable, and how far it is deliberate. As far as the sale of requirements is concerned, it may be taken as sufficiently proved that it is both. The marketing of produce is a much more complicated question.

Inter-trading in produce is growing, it would seem, at least as rapidly as the two movements which are parties to it, and from the foregoing analysis it may be said that there are certain demonstrable advantages to account for that growth and to promise its continuance. The elements of stability, quality, considerable scale of operations, efficiency resulting from the elimination of unnecessary agents, and commercial honesty and soundness are all usually characteristic of co-operative trade. These qualities may also be found in private undertakings, but the fact that they are so generally associated with co-operation shows that it is justifying itself simply as a commercial method; that in consequence it is generally considered desirable to do business with co-operative societies, and that this desirability is mutually recognised by the co-operative societies themselves.

But it may also be asked whether there is any further motive for inter-relations, and whether in particular the fact that both sides are co-operatively organised should lead to closer connection between them. It is natural that two bodies conducted on the same principles, and convinced that these principles have not only a commercial but a social value warranting their universal adoption, should incline to deal with one another, though this inclination alone would not support a lasting trade. Further, it has been pointed out that any organisation that increases the effective demand of the mass of consumers is indirectly benefiting agricultural producers, while anything that increases agricultural production does a like service for the consumer.

But it is obvious that the two movements, as producers and consumers, are also economically opposed. This may be felt so keenly that the co-operative producer finds himself, temporarily at least, more in sympathy with the private producer than the co-operative consumer, and the co-operative consumer doubts whether the co-operative producer or the private distributor is the more to be feared. Consumer and producer are mutually indispensable, but a conflict remains, centring round the idea of the just price mentioned already at the beginning of this study. In the co-operative movement both sides are professedly, and probably in fact, anxious to obtain the just price and no more, but both are anxious to determine the just price themselves. It becomes for each a question whether they will not be more likely to have their way if the other side is weak and divided, or, in other words, non-co-operative. Thus, from a commercial point of view, it is sometimes argued that an industrial society gets, for a time, a better bargain if it purchases its supplies from a number of small farmers rather than from a properly run co-operative society, and that a producers' organisation realises its highest prices through the competition of private dealers.

But it is necessary to take a wider view. The tendency of modern commerce is towards combination, trustification, cartels, rings, and so forth, and weak and disunited opponents are becoming harder to find. There exists already on both sides of the market a strong co-operative nucleus offering to co-operative customers the advantages and attractions already described. All previous combination had taken place on one side or the other of the consumer-producer frontier, not across it, the price continuing unstable to the disadvantage of both parties, unless one secured an overwhelming preponderance; in which case it ceased to be just, at least in the eyes of the other.

The peculiar service which co-operation can do to economic life in general, and to its own constituents in particular, is to place the relations of consumers and producers on an organised basis, and thence approach to a solution of the just price. No one claims that this has been completely achieved, but an advance has been made whose furthest point is marked by the various joint organisations, of which some account has been given. There are also organisations which, without forming a distinct joint body, carry on a counter-trade, and pay dividends on their purchases from one another. Thus a method has been found of dividing the profit or surplus which arises from all successful trading in a roughly equitable manner; more especially in the case of joint organisations the alliance gives each party a direct interest in the success of the other, while it places each in a strong position when dealing with its rivals in private trade. It tends also to a stabilisation of the market which is a public as well as a co-operative benefit. Whenever two co-operative organisations deal directly with one another, the superfluous speculator and middleman are eliminated, and with them unnecessary additions to the price. The situation is clarified by the removal of all persons benefiting from the transactions, except the primary producer and the ultimate consumer. With the formation of joint organisations the final and crucial problem of price begins to be tackled. It is along the lines of joint organisation between co-operative bodies of equal strength, and therefore incapable of overbearing one another, that the most valuable progress may be anticipated.

The ultimate purpose of co-operation is to prevent the wastage of social wealth by misdistribution. The more completely it can organise itself, the more completely will this purpose be achieved, and inter-trading is a step in the direction of complete organisation. One immediate benefit —stability of the market—has already been indicated. Further, if any part of world trade can be carried on more efficiently than before, there is an undoubted gain. But more specific suggestions have been made. It has been said, for instance, that inter-trading will lead to " rationalisation " in the sense advocated by the Economic Conference of the League of Nations. Co-operative organisation does undoubtedly eliminate waste of labour in unnecessary handling and leakage of wealth in speculation and to needless middlemen, and the more complete the organisation the more thoroughly will this be done. But co-operative business is to-day big business, and geographical rationalisation—a movement towards the consumption of local produce locally —is less likely to be attained or even sought by big centralised organisations. Indeed, in co-operative experience it seems as if the advantages of geographical rationalisation are outweighed by those of centralisation and the efficiency which results.

Perhaps the most important benefit which inter-relations are expected to confer is the reduction of the consumer-producer price spread. It may be said at once that no dramatic reduction in prices is likely to ensue immediately from such transactions. A marketing society may, and frequently does, secure for the farmer a better price for his produce. Sometimes the increase is considerable, sometimes a steady market is sought rather than enlarged profits. The consumers' society, on the other hand, rarely sells below current rates; its price reductions are cautious, and it prefers to make a surplus, which is distributed to customers as dividend on purchase. The agricultural society has in most cases its corresponding dividend on sales, and it is through these distributions that the real reduction in price spread is affected. Where the societies are in a strong position and find their surplus becoming permanent, they begin to adjust prices for their members' benefit. This affects the outside market also to the advantage of the non-co-operative public, but direct benefit will undoubtedly be confined to actual members of the co-operative movements.

Inter-trading is an element in the commercial success which is the indispensable factor in co-operative expansion, but the ultimate aims of co-operation are concerned as much with social economy as with commerce. It seeks to expand till it has transformed the whole of society to its own ideal economic and ethical form. In this social character the movement can admit no irreparable division in the interests of mankind nor any economic problem which co-operative principles and co-operative technique cannot solve. The problem of producers' and consumers' relations is one of the hardest confronting the co-operative movement; a solution of that problem, in which much progress has already been made, would crown all its economic achievements.

INDEX

For Product Safety Concerns and Information please contact our EU
representative GPSR@taylorandfrancis.com
Taylor & Francis Verlag GmbH, Kaufingerstraße 24, 80331 München, Germany